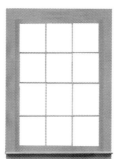

How to Dress
a Naked Window

Donna Babylon

**krause
publications**

700 E. State Street • Iola, WI 54990-0001

Published by

krause publications

700 E.State Street • Iola, WI 54990-0001
Telephone: 715/445/2214

Please call or write for our free catalog of publications.
Our toll-free number to place an order or obtain a free catalog is
800-258-0929 or
please use our regular business telephone 715-445-2214 for editorial
comment and further information.

Designed by Publication Design, Inc.

Photography by T.R. Wailes

Illustrations by Ann Davis Nunemacher

Watercolor renderings by Karen Janssen

Photos styled by Stacy Michell

Set construction by Dick Reese

Photography Studio: Daddy's Garage

Samples for photography made by Sheila Zent and Jean Fidler

p. 2, Woven-Buttonhole Valance
hardware: Design Trends® by Kirsch
paint: Sherwin Williams
tasseled tiebacks: Hollywood Trim™ by Dritz

p. 6, String Valance
fabric: Cyrus Clark

p. 9, Layered Valance
hardware: Studio Coordinates™ by Kirsch
paint: Sherwin Williams

p. 13, Flip-Over Valance
hardware: The Buckingham™ Collection by Kirsch
fabrics: Waverly
fringe trim: Waverly
wallpaper: Eisenhart Wallcoverings Co.

p. 17, Kick-Pleat Valance
fabric: Waverly
paint: Sherwin Williams
wallpaper border: Eisenhart Wallcoverings Co.
covered button forms: Prym/Dritz

p. 21, Cluster-Pleat Valance
hardware: Interior Expressions™ by Dritz
covered button forms: Prym/Dritz
wallpaper: Eisenhart Wallcovering Co.
Sew-in Multi-Pocket Pleater Tape: Prym/Dritz

p. 23, Tabbed Roman Shade
hardware: Studio Coordinates™ by Kirsch
fabric: Covington
paint: Sherwin Williams
giraffes and mask: SERRV International Gift Shop

p. 33, Cord-and-Eyelet Tab Curtain
hardware: Interior Expressions™ by Dritz
wallpaper: Eisenhart Wallcovering Co.
eyelets: Prym/Dritz
cording: Hollywood Trim™ by Dritz

p. 36, Contrasting-Buttonhole Tab Curtain
hardware: Interior Expressions™ by Dritz
wallpaper: Eisenhart Wallcovering Co.

p. 39, Shaped Tab Curtain
hardware: Interior Expressions™ by Dritz
wallpaper: Eisenhart Wallcovering Co.
covered button forms: Prym/Dritz

p. 42, Gathered Tab Curtain
fabric: Covington Fabrics
paint: Sherwin Williams

p. 48, Pinch-Pleat Draperies and Swag Scarf
hardware: Interior Expressions™ by Dritz
wallpaper: Eisenhart Wallcovering Co.
Sew-in Perfect Pleater Tape: Prym/Dritz

p. 53, Pinafore Curtain
hardware: Graber's Iron Artistry™ Collection
wallpaper border: Eisenhart Wallcoverings Co.
covered button forms: Prym/Dritz

p. 57, Attached Jabot Valance
hardware: Studio Coordinates™ by Kirsch
fabric: Covington
wallpaper: Eisenhart Wallcovering Co.

p. 62, Cuffed Curtain
hardware: Graber Wooden Pole Set
fabric: Cyrus Clark

p. 67, Knotted Scarf
hardware: Graber 1½" Dauphine Rod and Graber Pinnacle® Rod
fabric: Cyrus Clark

p. 72, Scalloped Valance
fabric: Covington
covered button forms: Prym/Dritz
wallpaper: Eisenhart Wallcovering Co.
holdbacks: Interior Expressions™ by Dritz

p. 78, Two-Tone Petal Valance
fabric: Covington
covered button forms: Prym/Dritz
wallpaper and border: Eisenhart Wallcovering Co.
paint: Sherwin Williams

p. 81, Pointed Valance
fabric: Schumacher
wallpaper and border: Eisenhart Wallcovering Co.
paint: Krylon® Living Color®

p. 84, Triangle Swag and Jabot
fabric: Covington
paint: Sherwin Williams

Manufactured in the United States of America

Library of Congress Cataloging-in-Publication Data

Babylon, Donna.
    How to dress a naked window / Donna Babylon
        p.   cm.
    Includes index.
    ISBN 0-8019-8743-1
    1.Drapery. 2.Drapery in interior decoration. 3.Sewing
I.Title
TT390.B26 1997
645'.3—dc21   96 51018
                                                            CIP

1 2 3 4 5 6 7 8 9 0   6 5 4 3 2 1 0 9 8 7

Contents

Acknowledgments

Whenever I do a book, especially the photo shoots, I keep a very hectic schedule. However, if it were not for my friends and family who unselfishly open their homes so I can find just the right props, the photographs would not happen. I want to especially thank my parents who not only let me turn their house topsy-turvy in my never-ending prop hunt, but provided Stacy and me with great meals. My aunt and uncle, Ruth and Charles Koontz, also tolerated my late night "raids" of their home. My friends Gale Bixler, Alice Hicks, and Tom and Marti Stansfield also let me root and rummage through their stuff, and I walked away with great finds. I also want to thank the employees at Babylon Vault Company who helped me move and store the sets, vacating and cleaning "the studio" and finding the obscure tools I always needed immediately.

Many companies generously provided me with products to use in this book. I would like to thank the following companies:

Covington Fabrics
15 E. 26th Street
New York, NY 10010

Cyrus Clark Fabrics
267 Fifth Avenue
New York, NY 10016

Eisenhart Wallcoverings Company
P. O. Box 464
Hanover, PA 17331

Graber Products, Springs Window Fashions Division
7549 Graber Road
Middletown, WI 53562

Kirsch
309 North Prospect Street
Sturgis, MI 49091

Krylon
31500 Solon Road
Solon, OH 44139

New Windsor Carryout, Inc.
105 Church Street
New Windsor, MD 21776

Prym/Dritz
P. O. Box 5028
Spartanburg, SC 29304

Schumacher
939 Third Avenue
New York, NY 10022

SERRV International Gift Shop
500 Main Street
New Windsor, MD 21776

Sherwin Williams (Westminster store)
901 E. Baltimore Boulevard
Westminster, MD 21157

Waverly Fabrics
79 Madison Avenue
New York, NY 10016

Introduction

I'm really glad you picked up this book. And because you did, I'm betting you have a bunch of naked windows just screaming to be dressed. Well, you've come to the right place. Contained in these pages are inspiration and instruction to help you put together the perfect window wardrobe.

Naked windows, huh? Well, if it makes you feel better, I talk to hundreds of people every year who are in the same situation. Their biggest question is: "What can I do with this window?" followed quickly by: "Are window treatments hard to make?" After answering these questions over and over, I thought it might be easier to write a book. (Not that I don't enjoy meeting all of you—but I'm beginning to sound like a broken record!) In brief, the answer to the first question is: "Let's see. . . " and the answer to the second is an emphatic "No!" Let me explain.

One of my goals for *How to Dress a Naked Window* was to feature designs that are easy to make and easy to visualize in your home. More importantly, I wanted to provide complete directions that are well written and easy to follow—including lots of illustrations to guide you along the way. I selected construction methods that produce professional-looking results with minimal aggravation. (Then I laid awake at night trying to translate these methods into easy-to-follow directions.) After a lot of trial and error and several edits, I have achieved my goals.

The bottom line is this: If you don't sew, this book is for you. If you do sew, this book is for you, too. As you leaf through its pages, you'll see that exciting and fun window treatments are not reserved for expensive decorators and upscale department stores. They're here. They're for you. And they're not needlessly complicated either. Just keep in mind that most window treatments are geometric shapes with straight-line sewing. Not an overwhelming combination, don't you agree?

To create a window treatment that's "just right" for your home, you've got to make some decisions. I've selected fun and fashionable fabrics for the examples shown, but don't limit yourself to my choices. Instead, adapt the treatments in the book to reflect your personality and to coordinate with your decor.

In each project, I walk you through the measuring, cutting, and sewing process. Then I explain how to hang the window treatments when they are complete. I have listed the supplies and tools with the proper names so that if you are like me—somewhat intimidated when walking into a hardware store—you'll at least be armed with the correct name for what you need. No more "thing-a-ma-jigs" or "doo-dads"! Leave your hardware-store jitters at the front door and ask confidently for "two toggle bolts, please."

My favorite part of the book is Chapter 5, entitled "General Instructions." This chapter is filled to the brim with wonderful tips, tricks, and helpful information that usually take years to learn. I've compiled them in one place in the hopes that you'll gain confidence and enthusiasm with each new technique you try.

As you can see, it's all here for you. This is the only book you'll ever need to make your own window decor. Then, if I ever have the chance to meet you, you won't have to ask "What can I do with my naked windows?" Instead, you'll be able to pull out some photos and show me those windows completely dressed!

Chapter 1

VALANCES

Woven-Buttonhole Valance

Show off fancy finials on a decorative rod with this simple treatment. Choosing the tasseled tiebacks or coordinating cord that will gather the fabric around each buttonhole is half the fun.

This treatment is a simple lined valance. The rod is woven in and out of buttonholes along the top edge, and cording or tasseled tiebacks are used to secure the gathers at each buttonhole.

Techniques to Know Before You Begin

Fabric Calculations

1. Mount the brackets 2 to 4" above the top edge of the window frame and 1 to 4" out from each side edge of the window frame. Place the rod in the brackets (Fig. 1).

2–4"

Figure 1

2. To determine the finished width of the valance, measure the length of the rod between the brackets and multiply this number by 2. From the following list, select the established finished width that is closest to the total: 70, 83, 96, 109, 122, 135, 148, 161. (The finished width must be one of these established widths so that the buttonhole placement falls correctly.)

3. To determine the cut width of the decora-tor fabric, add 4" to the suggested finished width you reached in Step 2.

4. To determine the cut width of the lining fabric, *subtract* 2" from the finished width in Step 2.

5. To determine the number of decorator fabric widths you need to achieve the cut width, divide the cut width of the decorator fabric, from Step 3, by the width of the fabric you are using. Round up to the next whole number.

6. To determine the number of lining fabric widths you need to achieve the cut width, divide the cut width of the lining fabric, from Step 4, by the width of the fabric you are using. Round up to the next whole number.

7. To determine the length, measure from the top of the rod to point on the window where you would like the valance to end. A good length is 16 to 18", but it can be any length that looks best on the window.

8. The cut length for each decorator fabric width is the above measurement plus 8".

9. The cut length for each lining fabric width is the measurement from Step 7 plus 5".

10. To calculate the total yardage of decorator fabric, multiply the cut length of the decorator fabric, from Step 8, by the number of widths you need, from Step 5. (If you need more than one fabric width and the fabric you have selected has a repeat, multiply the repeat distance by the number of widths and add this figure to the total. The extra fabric will allow you to match the designs.) Divide this num-ber by 36, and round up to the next ¼ yard.

11. To calculate the total yardage of lining fabric, multiply the cut length of the lining fabric, from Step 9, by the number of panels you need, from Step 6. Divide this number by 36, and round up to the next ¼ yard.

12. Use Fig. 5 to determine the amount of cording or tiebacks you need. You'll need one tieback or 30" of cording for each 8" section.

Cutting Instructions

1. Use a carpenter's square to straighten one end of both fabrics.

2. Cut decorator fabric widths to the cut length from Step 8 in Fabric Calculations; make sure the designs in the panels match exactly.

3. Cut lining widths to the cut length from Step 9 in Fabric Calculations.

Construction

Note: Use ¹/₂" seam allowances unless other-wise directed.

1. If you determined that more than one fabric width is needed to achieve the cut width, sew the decorator fabric panels and lining fabric panels together now. Trim, if necessary. Remember to avoid a center seam when stitching widths together. See Stitching Fabric Widths Together, page 97.

2. Hem the lining and decorator fabric separately. First, hem the decorator fabric with a double 3" hem. At the bottom of each panel of the decorator fabric, fold over and press 6" of fabric toward the wrong side. Tuck in the top of the hem 3" to meet the fold. Stitch or fuse the hem.

3. To hem the lining, create a double 2" hem, using the method in Step 2. Stitch or fuse the hem.

4. Place decorator fabric and lining right sides together. Pin together along one side seam. Make sure the top edge of the decorator fabric and lining fabric meet, and that the bottom edge of the lining is 1" shorter than the decorator fabric. Stitch one side seam together. Press the seam toward the lining.

5. Gently pull the lining over to meet the other side of the decorator fabric (Fig. 2).

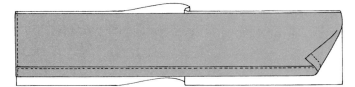

Figure 2

Pin this side seam together, and again, make sure the top edge of both fabrics are even and the bottom edge of the lining is 1" shorter than the decorator fabric. Stitch this side seam. Press the seam toward the lining.

6. With the decorator fabric and lining fabric still right sides together, place valance on a large work surface. Arrange valance so the decorator fabric "wraps" around to the lining side equally on each side, about 1½". Pin across the top edge to hold in place.

7. Stitch through all layers across the top edge of the valance (Fig. 3).

8. Clip top edge corners diagonally to eliminate bulk.

9. Turn valance right side out. Arrange the

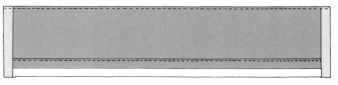

Figure 3

valance so the decorator fabric "wraps" around to the back equally along the entire length of each side edge, from the top of the valance to the bottom hem. Press side edges.

10. Create mitered corners (see Fig. 4). With wrong side facing you, diagonally fold the bottom corners of the side hem of the decorator fabric under at a 45° angle. The point of each corner should meet the side edge. Press. Hand stitch in place.

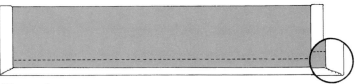

Figure 4

11. Mark the buttonhole placement along the top edge of the right side. Buttonholes are vertical and are 2" long; they begin 3¼" from the top. Buttonholes are alternately 5" and 8" apart (see Fig. 5). Begin by marking the fabric 5" in from one side and 3¼" down from the top edge. Mark the valance as indicated in Fig. 5, stopping at the finished width determined in Step 2 in Fabric Calculations. The last buttonhole mark should be 5" from the end.

Pins indicate buttonholes

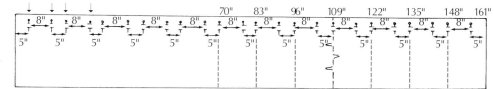

Figure 5

Shading Legend

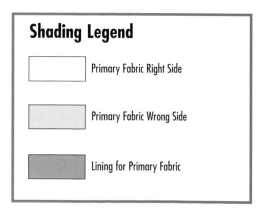

Primary Fabric Right Side

Primary Fabric Wrong Side

Lining for Primary Fabric

12. Make 2" vertical machine-made button-holes at each mark. Begin the top of the buttonhole at the 3¼" mark.

Installing and "Dressing" the Valance

1. Weave the rod in and out of buttonholes (Fig. 6).

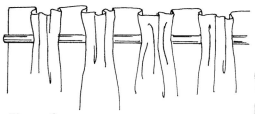

Figure 6

2. If using cording, cut it into 30" lengths.

3. Thread cording or tasseled tiebacks through buttonholes at top of rod. Tie into even bows (Fig. 7).

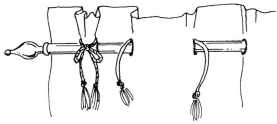

Figure 7

4. Place rod in brackets; adjust fullness if necessary. You may need to tighten or loosen the bows.

5. If necessary to prevent drooping, secure the edges of the header—the part just above where the rod is inserted—to the back of the rod with double-stick carpet tape.

Alternative Design

This woven-buttonhole heading is a great choice for floor-length curtains, too.

String Valance

Looking for a really easy window treatment? It doesn't get much simpler than this! Two lined rectangles are the basis for this unique design. And, yes, those are kitchen cabinet knobs functioning as decorative hangers for the valance. Self-fabric ties, cording, or ribbon are the "string" used to suspend the valance from the knobs.

This treatment uses two fabrics: a decorator fabric for the "right" side of the valance, and a coordinating fabric for the "lining" of the valance, which folds back. There are two panels per window. Hang the valance from either decorative cabinet knobs screwed into the window frame or a pegged shelf installed just above the top frame edge.

Techniques to Know Before You Begin

Installing the Hardware

1. Knobs are installed across the top of the window frame approximately 1" from the top. To determine the knob placement, measure the width of the window frame and mark the center with a pencil. Make two more marks ½" in from each side of the frame (see Fig. 1). Divide each half of the frame, from the center mark to each end mark, into even sections, and mark. Note: There should be at least four knobs on each side of the center knob; the total number of knobs must be an odd number.

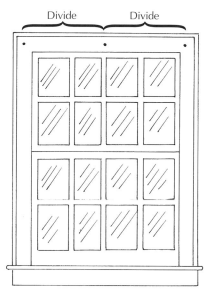

Divide   Divide

Figure 1

2. Drill a hole at each of these marks. (You need to drill a hole to avoid splintering the wooden frame.)

3. Insert machine end (flat tip) of hanger bolt into knob. Screw knob into hole.

TIP: Instead of using kitchen knobs, you can install a Shaker-style peg shelf above the window frame and hang the valance from the pegs.

Fabric Calculations

Note: The following calculations are for both the decorator fabric and the coordinating fabric.

1. To determine the cut width of both fabrics, measure the width of the window from outside frame to outside frame. Multiply this figure by 2 (for adequate fullness), and add 1" for seam allowances.

2. To determine how many widths you will need for each panel, divide the cut width by the width of the fabric you are using. Round up to the next whole number.

3. To determine the finished length, measure the distance from the knobs to the point on the window where you would like the valance to end.

4. The cut length of the valance is the finished length plus 1" for seam allowances.

5. To determine the total yardage of decorator fabric, multiply the cut length by the number of widths you determined you need in Step 2. (If you need more than one fabric width and the fabric you have selected has a repeat, multiply the repeat distance by the number of widths and add this figure to the total. The extra fabric will allow you to match the designs.) Divide by 36 and round up to the next ¼ yard.

6. Purchase an equal amount of coordinating fabric for the lining.

7. Determine the yardage of cording for the tabs. Take the total number of knobs, and add three—for the two tabs at the bottom inside corners, and an extra length because both inside tabs hang from the center knob. Multiply this number by four. (The length of each tab is 4".) Divide the total by 36.

Construction

Note: Use ½" seam allowances unless otherwise noted.

1. Straighten one end of both of the fabrics with a carpenter's square.

2. Determine the finished dimensions of each half of the valance. The finished width of each half is equal to the width of the window from outside frame to outside frame. The finished length was determined in Step 3 in Fabric Calculations.

3. The cut width of each half is equal to the finished width plus 1" for seam allowances.

4. The cut length was determined in Step 4 in Fabric Calculations.

5. Cut both decorator and lining fabrics to their cut length; make sure the designs in the widths match exactly.

Materials Needed

From the Fabric Store
- Decorator fabric for valance (Select a medium-weight, 54"-wide decorator fabric, such as broadcloth, chintz, damask, denim, linen, or sateen.)
- Coordinating decorator fabric for lining. (See guidelines for decorator fabric)
- Thread to match decorator fabrics
- Ribbon or decorative cording for string tabs, ½" wide
- Dressmaker scissors

- Fabric marking pen or pencil

From the Hardware Store
- Decorative cabinet knobs, 1⅛" diameter. (Or, choose unpainted wooden knobs and paint them to match the fabric or window frame.)
- Hanger bolts, 1" long. 8-32 or 10-32, depending on knob. One bolt for each knob
- Electric or hand drill with bit to fit hanger bolts
- Carpenter's square
- *Optional:* Level

6. If you determined in Step 2 in Fabric Calculations that more than one fabric width is needed, sew the decorator fabric widths together and the lining widths together now. If necessary, trim widths to achieve the exact cut width. Remember to avoid a center seam when stitching widths together. See Stitching Fabric Widths Together, page 97.

7. Cut cording for tabs into 4" lengths.

8. Determine tab placement along the top edge of the decorator fabric. Measure in

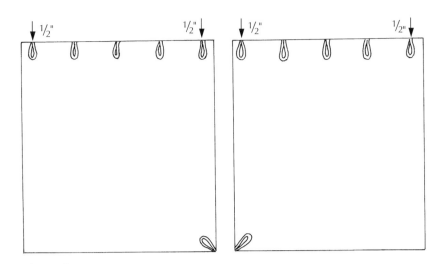

Figure 3

1/2" from each side edge and mark with pins (see Fig. 2). To mark the placement for the remaining tabs, fold the fabric into sections and mark each fold. For example, if there are five tabs per panel, fold the fabric into four sections; for seven tabs, fold the fabric into six sections. Mark each division point with a pin. *Important:* Each panel will have the same number of tabs and the tabs at each edge will be 1/2" in from the edge.

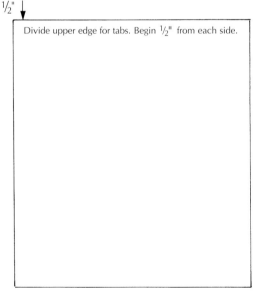

Divide upper edge for tabs. Begin 1/2" from each side.

Figure 2

9. Position the tabs by laying the decorator fabric right side up on a large, flat work surface. Fold each tab in half. Place the ends even with the top edge of fabric at each mark (Fig. 3). Place a tab diagonally at the two bottom inside corners of the fabric. Pin tabs in place.

10. Place lining and decorator fabrics right sides together. Stitch around all four sides; leave an 8" opening along one long side for turning (see Fig. 4). For reinforcement, stitch again along top edge where tabs are enclosed.

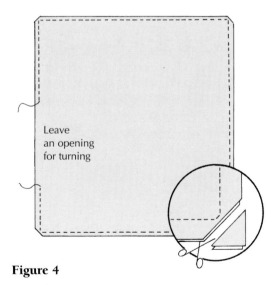

Leave an opening for turning

Figure 4

11. Clip all corners diagonally to eliminate bulk.

12. Turn valance right sides out, hand stitch or fuse the opening closed. Press smooth.

Installing the Valance

1. Place tabs over knob. The tab at the inside edge of both panels hang on the center knob. Bring up the center front corners and place over outside knobs.

2. Adjust folds as desired.

Layered Valance

This clever valance does not use much yardage, so go ahead and splurge on a fabric you really love. Then add drama by choosing a stark contrasting color for the bottom layer. Coordinating tassels and cording are the perfect finishing touches.

Small pieces of wire inserted in each end of this valance allow the returns to bend back and hang perpendicular to the wall. The two bent edges (not visible in this photo) create the effect of a cornice. This treatment uses two layers of coordinating fabrics, each of them lined.

Fabric Calculations

1. Mount the brackets 2 to 4" above the top edge of the window frame and 1 to 4" out from each side edge of the window frame. Place the rod in the brackets (Fig. 1).

2. To determine the cut width of both layers of the valance and of the lining, first measure the length of the rod between the brackets. Next, measure the return—the distance that the bracket extends from the wall—on each side. Add the three measurements together, and then add 1" for seam allowances to get the total.

Figure 1

3. To determine how many fabric widths you need to achieve the cut width, divide the cut width, from Step 2, by the width of fabric you are using. Round up to the next whole number.

4. To determine the cut length for the under layer and its lining, measure from the top edge of the window frame to the desired finished length of the under layer (the black portion in the photograph). Add 1" for seam allowances to this number. The cut length of the top layer of the valance and its lining is 3" shorter.

5. To find out the total yardage for each fabric, multiply the cut length by the number of widths you need, from Step 3. (If you need more than one fabric width and the fabric you have selected has a repeat, multiply the repeat distance by the number of widths and add this figure to the total. The extra fabric will allow you to match the designs.) Divide this number by 36 and round up to the next ¼ yard. Repeat these calculations for the lining of each layer.

6. To determine the finished length of the tabs, drape a string over the rod and pin it together where the top edge of the shade will be. Note: The top edge of the shade should be slightly above the top edge of the window frame. Mark the string before removing it from the rod and measure the distance between the marks.

7. To determine the cut length of each cording tab, add 1" for seam allowances to the finished length.

8. The end tabs are placed at each return mark, not at the very edge of the valance. The remaining tabs are spaced every 4 to 6" to avoid having the fabric "droop" between tabs. (You decide the exact distance apart of the tabs.) So, to calculate the number of tabs you need, divide the measurement of the area between the returns by the number of inches apart the tabs are spaced, and round this figure up to the next whole number.

9. To determine the total yardage of cording tabs, multiply the cut length of the tab by the number of tabs you need, and divide by 36.

Creating the Pattern

1. Make a paper pattern for each layer. First, make a pattern for the under layer. Tape the tracing paper together into a rectangle shape equal to the finished dimensions of the under layer. (The finished dimensions are the cut width by the cut length, minus the ½" for seam allowances from each edge.)

2. Along each side of the pattern, mark the return measurement. Draw a vertical line from the top to the bottom of the rectangle along each side. Be sure to transfer these marks onto the wrong side of the fabric and the lining. Also mark the exact center of the rectangle to use as a reference point when you create the bottom edge.

3. Begin at the center and work toward each side. With a ruler, draw a jagged edge that is visually pleasing, stopping at the mark for the return measurement. (Be sure the bottom edge of the return area is a horizontal straight line, as shown in Fig. 2.) Cut away the

---

Materials Needed

From the Fabric Store
- Decorator fabric for the top layer (Select a medium-weight, 54"-wide decorator fabric, such as broadcloth, chintz, damask, denim, linen, or sateen.)
- Coordinating fabric for the under layer. (See guidelines for decorator fabric.)
- Lining fabric for both the top and bottom layers
- Thread to match decorator fabrics
- Decorative cording for the tabs
- Coordinating tassels, approximately 3" long, one for each interior point
- Dressmaker scissors
- Large pieces of tracing paper for the pattern
- Point turner
- Decorative rod, finials, and brackets (also available at department and hardware stores)
- Fabric marking pen or pencil
- *Optional:* Bias binding

From the Hardware Store
- Six 8" lengths of bell wire (you can ask for it by that name, it's the wire used in doorbells)
- Metal measuring tape
- Carpenter's square
- *Optional:* Double-stick carpet tape

excess paper along this line. Then, tape the pattern in place on the rod. Stand back and see if you like the look you created! Tip 1: You may find it helpful to draw the pattern to scale on graph paper before you begin. Tip 2: If you want the design to be symmetrical, fold the paper in half vertically, and draw the jagged edges from the center to the return mark. Cut through both layers of the paper pattern along the jagged edges. Open out the pattern to see the finished design.

4. Make a pattern for the top layer of the valance. Trace the pattern for the under layer onto another piece of paper, but make this pattern 3" shorter at the top.

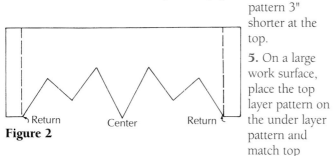

Figure 2

5. On a large work surface, place the top layer pattern on the under layer pattern and match top edges. Examine the relationship between the angles and the layers. You may need to adjust some of the angles for better visual proportion. Also, lay the tassels on each interior point of the top layer to make sure they don't hang below the under layer (see photo). Make any adjustments to the paper pattern now.

Construction

Note: All seam allowances are ¹/₂" unless otherwise noted.

1. Straighten one end of all fabrics using a carpenter's square.

2. Cut the decorator and lining fabrics into lengths determined in Step 4 in Fabric Calculations; make sure designs in fabric lengths match exactly.

3. If you determined in Step 3 in Fabric Calculations that more than one width is needed to achieve the cut width, sew the decorator fabric widths together and the lining fabric widths together now. Trim if necessary. Remember to avoid a center seam when stitching widths together. See Stitching Fabric Widths Together, page 97.

4. Using the pattern for the top layer, cut one shape from the decorator fabric, and one shape from the lining fabric (Fig. 3). *Important: Add ¹/₂" seam allowance around the entire perimeter when cutting the fabric!*

5. Using the pattern for the under layer, cut one shape from the coordinating decorator fabric, and one shape from the lining fabric.

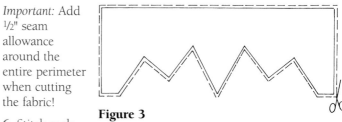

Figure 3

Important: Add ¹/₂" seam allowance around the entire perimeter when cutting the fabric!

6. Stitch each layer separately by placing each decorator fabric and its lining right sides together. Stitch down one side, along the bottom edge and up the other side; leave the top edge open for turning (Fig. 4).

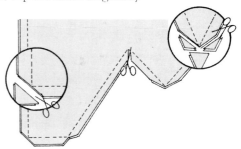

Figure 4

7. To eliminate bulk along the bottom jagged edge, trim the seam allowances to ¹/₄". Also, at each inside point, clip the fabric diagonally and cut away small notches of fabric (Fig. 5).

8. To add the bell wire to the bottom edge, make a small, closed loop at each end of the wire to keep the wire from poking through the fabric. Lay the wire along side the stitching line in the seam allowance starting in the corner (see Fig. 6). The wire should be long enough to "cross" the vertical return mark so that the return has something to "bend against," as shown. Set the machine to a wide zigzag stitch. Carefully stitch over the wire; be careful not to hit the wire with the needle or the needle may break.

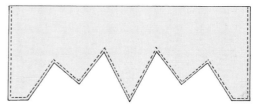

Figure 5

9. Turn both layers right side out. Using a point turner, push the fabric out from the inside to create sharp points. Press along the seam so the lining and decorator fabric are equally divided and neither shows on the opposite side.

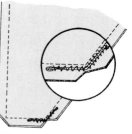

Figure 6

10. Determine and mark the placement of the tabs along the top edge of the top layer. The first and last tab are placed at each return mark, not at the very edge of the valance, as shown in Fig. 7. The remaining tabs are spaced every 4 to 6" apart between the first and last tab. Mark the position of each tab with a fabric marking pen or pencil.

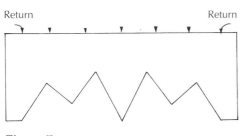

Figure 7

11. Cut the cording into the determined tab length, from Step 7 in Fabric Calculations.

12. Fold the cording in half so the cut edges are even and side by side. Pin cording in place to the fabric side of the top layer of the valance (Fig. 8).

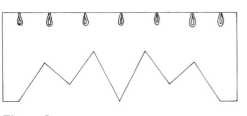

Figure 8

13. Place the fabric side of the top layer to the lining side of the under layer; align the top edges.

14. Stitch through all layers across the top edge of valance (Fig. 9). For reinforcement, stitch again over each tab.

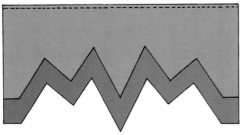

Figure 9

15. Clean finish this seam by serging, overcast stitching, or enclosing the seam in bias tape.

16. Insert the bell wire into the top corners of the valance by laying the wire against the stitching line (in the seam allowance) perpendicular to the return mark, starting in the

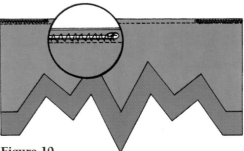

Figure 10

corner (see Fig. 10). Set the machine to a wide zigzag stitch. Carefully stitch over the wire; be careful not to hit the wire with the needle or the needle may break.

17. Turn the top layer to the outside. Hand stitch tassels to each interior point of the top layer.

Installing and "Dressing" the Valance

1. Lay the valance on a large work surface, right sides down. Carefully fold back each return toward the lining side of the valance, as shown in Fig. 11.

2. Place the valance on the rod, making sure the top seam is straight.

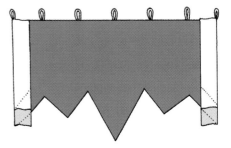

Figure 11

3. Now open up the return area so it forms a right angle and is perpendicular to the wall (Fig. 12). If necessary, secure the return to the window frame with double-stick carpet tape.

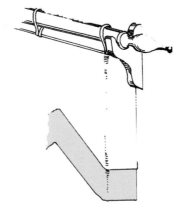

Figure 12

Flip-Over Valance

Fringe and covered cording add custom touches to this formal treatment. Select just the right hardware, like the beautiful rod shown here, and you will create a timeless window treatment that is sure to garner compliments from your family and friends.

Techniques to Know Before You Begin

This layered window treatment requires two coordinating fabrics. The top layer of the valance uses a patterned decorative fabric and decorative fringe trim, the bottom layer uses a solid coordinating fabric and decorative piping, which you can purchase or make yourself. Each layer is lined.

Fabric Calculations

Note: Mount brackets 2 to 4" above top edge of the window frame and 1 to 4" out from each side edge of the window frame. Place rod in brackets (Fig. 1).

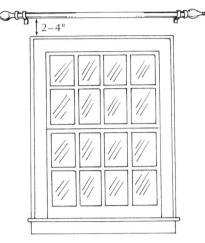

2 – 4"

Figure 1

BOTTOM LAYER

1. To determine the finished width of the bottom layer of the valance, measure the length of the rod between the brackets.

2. To determine the cut width of the bottom layer of the valance, add 1", for seam allowances, to the finished width.

3. To determine the number of fabric widths you need for the cut width of the bottom layer, divide the cut width by the width of fabric you are using. Round up to the next whole number.

4. To determine the finished length for the bottom layer, measure from the top of the rod to the point on the window where you would like the center point to fall (the burgundy portion in the photograph).

5. To determine the cut length for the bottom layer add ¾" to the finished length for seam and take-up allowances.

6. To obtain the total yardage of solid coordinating fabric for the bottom layer, multiply the cut length by the number of widths needed, from Step 3. Divide this number by 36 and round up to next ¼ yard. You need this same amount of lining fabric for the lining of the bottom layer.

7. After the pattern is drafted, measure the two vertical edges and the two diagonal edges to determine the amount of cording needed.

TOP LAYER

1. To determine the finished width of the top layer, take the finished width of the bottom layer from Step 1 under instructions for the Bottom Layer, and subtract 4". (The top layer is 4" narrower than the bottom layer.)

2. To determine the cut width of the top layer, take the finished width of this layer and add 1" for seam allowances.

3. To determine the number of fabric widths you need for the cut width of the top layer, divide the cut width by the width of fabric you are using. Round up to next whole number.

4. The finished length of the top layer of the valance is 2" shorter than the finished length of the bottom layer, from Step 4 in instructions for Fabric Calculations—Bottom Layer.

5. The cut length of the top layer of the valance is 2" shorter than the cut length of the bottom layer.

6. To obtain the total yardage necessary for the decorative fabric, multiply the cut length by the number of widths needed from Step 3. (If you need more than one fabric width and the fabric you have selected has a repeat, multiply the repeat distance by the number of widths and add this figure to the total. The extra fabric will allow you to match the designs). Divide this number by 36 and round up to next ¼ yard. You need this same amount of lining fabric for the lining of the top layer, minus the extra yard for the cording. Note: If making your own cording for bottom layer, you need an additional 1 yard of patterned decorative fabric to cover the cording.

7. After the pattern is drafted, measure the two diagonal edges to determine amount of fringe trim needed.

Creating the Pattern

Note: To help you plan the valance, you can use graph paper to draw the valance to scale.

1. Make a full-size paper pattern for each layer. Tape tracing paper together into two rectangle shapes equal to the exact finished dimensions—the finished width by the finished length—of each layer of the valance.

Materials Needed

From the Fabric Store
- Decorator fabric for the top layer (Select a medium-weight 54"-wide decorator fabric, such as broadcloth, chintz, damask, denim, linen, sateen, or tapestry.)
- Coordinating fabric for the under layer. (See guidelines for decorator fabric.)
- Lining for both the top and bottom layers
- Thread to match decorator fabrics
- Decorative fringe trim to coordinate with fabrics for

bottom edge of valance (1" long)
- Cording or ready-made piping for bottom edges of valance (5/32")
- Dressmaker scissors
- Large pieces of tracing paper for pattern
- Fabric marking pen or pencil
- Point turner
- Decorative rod, finials, and brackets (also available at hardware and department stores)

From the Hardware Store
- Carpenter's square

2. Mark the exact center of each rectangle along the top and bottom edges. Use this mark as a reference point when you draft the bottom edge.

3. Along each side of each paper pattern, measure and mark 6½" up from the bottom (see Fig. 2). Draw a diagonal line from the bottom center mark to each side mark. Cut along these lines.

4. Center the smaller pattern directly on top of the larger pattern (see Fig. 3). Match center marks on the top edge and make sure top edges are even (the top layer will be shorter). Tape top edges together. Place paper pattern over rod; the "seam" should be slightly down the backside of the rod. Stand back and see if you like the look you created. Adjust dimensions if necessary. Remember, the paper pattern is the *finished* width and length. Keep in mind that the top layer has fringe.

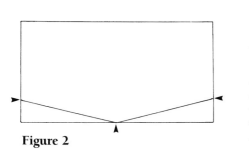

Figure 2

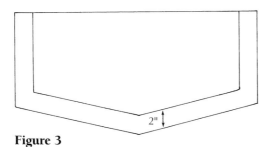

Figure 3

Construction

Note: All seam allowances are ½" unless otherwise noted.

1. Cut the decorator and lining fabrics into lengths determined in Step 5 in Fabric Calculations; make sure designs in fabric lengths match exactly.

2. If you determined that you need more than one fabric width to achieve the cut widths of the layers, sew all of the fabric widths together and lining widths together now, and trim if necessary. Remember to avoid a center seam when stitching widths together. See Stitching Fabric Widths Together, page 97.

3. Untape the patterns. Using the pattern for the top layer, cut one shape from the decorative fabric, and one layer from the lining fabric. *Important:* Add ½" seam allowance

around entire perimeter when cutting fabric!

4. Using the pattern for the bottom layer, cut one shape from the coordinating fabric, and one layer from the lining fabric. *Important:* Add ½" seam allowance around entire perimeter when cutting fabric!

5. If you are making your own piping, cut 1¼"-wide bias strips.

6. Place decorator fabric for top layer right side up on a large work surface. Baste fringe along diagonal sides so that the bottom of the fringe faces the top edge of the valance (Fig. 4). Place lining fabric directly on top of decorator fabric; match all edges.

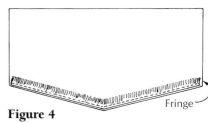

Figure 4

Fringe

7. Stitch around four sides: both vertical sides and two diagonal sides (Fig. 5). Leave the top edge open for turning.

8. Prepare fabric-covered cording (see Make Your Own Piping, p. 100).

Alternative Design

Try sizing the valance pattern so you can fit several on the same rod. Then use the multiple valances over a fabric shade or mini blinds.

Figure 5

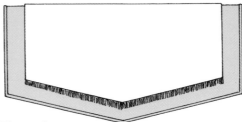

Figure 6

9. Place coordinating fabric for bottom layer right side up on a large, flat surface. Baste cording along vertical and diagonal sides. Place right side of lining fabric directly on top of decorator fabric; match all edges.

10. Stitch around four sides: both vertical sides and two diagonal sides. Leave the top edge open for turning.

11. Along the bottom edge of both layers, clip the fabric diagonally at the point.

12. Turn both layers right side out. Using a point turner, push the fabric out from the inside to create sharp points. Press smooth.

13. Center the right side of the top layer to the lining side of the bottom layer; align top edges. The bottom layer should extend evenly from the vertical and diagonal sides of the top layer.

14. Stitch through all layers across the top edge.

15. Clean finish this seam by either serging, overcast stitching, or enclosing the seam in bias tape. Turn valance so that lining side of top layer faces fabric side of under layer (Fig. 6).

16. *Optional:* Hand stitch tassel to the end of point on top layer.

Installing and "Dressing" the Valance

1. Place valance over rod; the seam of the valance should be slightly down the backside of the rod, and obscured by the rod.

2. To hold side extensions in place, secure them to rod with double-faced tape or hook-and-loop tape (Fig. 7).

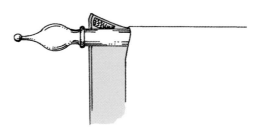

Figure 7

Kick-Pleat Valance

Feel free to kick up your heels when you find out how easy it is to make this valance. The "pleats" are created by arranging separate lined rectangles of fabric over a valance base. Covered buttons that "kick up" the edges are a clever decorator touch.

Techniques to Know Before You Begin

This valance is made up of two layers. The under layer is a fitted, lined valance. The top layer is composed of individual rectangles—or flaps—of fabric that are sewn, one at a time, to the under layer. Pulling back the bottom corners of the rectangles reveals the under layer.

Materials Needed

From the Fabric Store

- Decorator fabric for the top layer (Select a medium-weight 54"-wide decorator fabric, such as broadcloth, chintz, damask, linen, or sateen.)
- Coordinating fabric for the under layer, which is also used as lining for the top layer. (See guidelines for decorator fabrics.)
- Lining fabric for bottom layer
- Thread to match decorator fabrics
- Covered button forms, 1⅛" diameter
- Large pieces of tracing paper to plan flaps

- Dressmaker scissors
- Fabric marking pen or pencil
- Point turner
- Drapery weights, 4 per valance

From the Hardware Store

- 1 × 4" wood mounting board
- Angle brackets (at least 2, and then 1 for every 36" of finished width)
- Screws, 2" long (2–4 for every angle bracket)
- Heavy-duty staple gun with ½" staples
- Metal measuring tape
- Carpenter's square
- Push pins

Planning the Valance

1. Determine the length of the mounting board. If the window has a frame, measure the width of the window from outside frame edge to outside frame edge, and add 1". If the window does not have a frame, measure the opening, and add 2".

2. Prepare mounting board by either painting it to match the wall color or by covering the board with decorator fabric.

3. Install the mounting board 2 to 4" above the window like a shelf; secure angle brackets to the wall, and rest mounting board on them, as shown in Fig. 1. Note: Do not yet permanently attach the board to the brackets, as you will need it later when attaching the valance.

4. The finished width of the under layer of the valance is equal to the length of the mounting board plus the returns.

5. To determine the finished length of the under layer and flaps, measure from the top edge of the board to the point on the window where you would like the valance to end. A good finished length is 16 to 18", but it can be any length that looks best on the window.

6. Decide how many flaps

you would like across the front of the board. Generally, an odd number of flaps is more visually pleasing than an even number. The minimum width of each flap is 10".

7. To determine the width of each flap, divide the length of the front edge of the mounting board by the number of flaps you would like. Be sure the resulting width is 10" or greater.

TIP: The fabric you select for the flaps may help you determine the width of each flap. For example, the fabric may have a luscious rose motif that demands to be centered in each flap, or a striped fabric may have a particular section that catches your eye.

Making the Patterns for the Flaps

Note: Do not include any seam allowances in these patterns; they will be added when the flaps are cut out.

1. Make full-size paper patterns for each of the front flaps. Each pattern should be a rectangle equal to the width of the flap, from Step 7 in Planning the Valance, by the finished length of the valance, from Step 5 in Planning the Valance.

2. Make patterns for the two flaps that will cover the returns, or side edges. Measure the width of the returns. The patterns should be rectangles equal to the width of the return by the finished length of the valance.

3. Make sure the total widths of all the flaps are equal to the finished width of the valance. Use push pins to attach all the patterns to the board to double-check. Also, pin the patterns for the returns to the board to double-check the widths of the return patterns.

Fabric Calculations

Note: This layered window treatment requires two coordinating fabrics. The under layer uses contrasting fabric and is lined with lining fabric. However the top flaps, made of decorator fabric, are lined with the same contrasting fabric used for the under layer.

FRONT FLAPS — DECORATOR FABRIC

1. The easiest way to determine the yardage of decorator fabric is to take the flap patterns to the fabric store. Match plaids, stripes, and motifs if necessary. Remember, you will need an extra ½" on all sides of the flap patterns for seam allowances.

2. If you plan to cover the mounting board with decorator fabric, be sure to include the amount you will need to do this is in the total yardage.

UNDER LAYER — CONTRASTING FABRIC

1. To determine the cut width of the under

2–4"

Figure 1

layer, first measure the length of the board. Next, measure both returns. Add these three figures together, and then 1¼" for seam allowances and ease.

2. To determine the number of fabric widths you need for the cut width of the under layer, divide the cut width by the width of fabric you are using. Round up to the next whole number.

3. To determine the cut length of the under layer, take the finished length from Step 5 in Planning the Valance, and add 1" to this number for seam allowances.

4. To determine the total yardage of the contrasting fabric—used for both the under layer and the lining of the flaps, multiply the cut length by the number of widths needed. (If you need more than one fabric width and the fabric you have selected has a repeat, multiply the repeat distance by the number of widths and add this figure to the total. The extra fabric will allow you to match the designs.) Divide this number by 36. Add to this the extra yardage for the flaps, (use the method in Step 1 in Fabric Calculations—Front Flaps). Round up to the next ¼ yard.

5. To determine the total yardage of lining fabric for the under layer, multiply the cut length of the under layer by the number of panels needed. Divide this number by 36 and round up to next ¼ yard.

Construction

FLAPS—DECORATOR
CONTRASTING FABRICS
Note: All seam allowances are ¹/₂".

1. Before you begin construction, straighten one end of the decorator fabric, contrasting fabric and lining fabric using a carpenter's square.

2. Pin paper patterns to the right side of decorator fabric. Cut around each shape. *Important:* Add ½" for seam allowance around entire perimeter of rectangle when cutting fabric!

3. Pin paper patterns to the right side of contrasting fabric. Cut around each shape. *Important:* Add ½" for seam allowance around entire perimeter of rectangle when cutting fabric!

4. For each flap, place decorator fabric and lining fabric right sides together. Stitch around three sides; leave top edge open for turning (Fig. 2).

5. Clip bottom corners diagonally to eliminate bulk.

6. Turn the flaps right side out. Using a point

turner, push the fabric out from the inside to create sharp points. Press smooth.

7. Insert one drapery weight into each bottom corner of the two flaps that cover the return area. If needed, secure weight to lining with a few hand stitches.

Figure 2

8. Clean finish the top edge of each flap by either serging, overcast stitching, or enclosing the seam in bias binding.

UNDER LAYER—CONTRASTING FABRIC
Note: All seam allowances are ¹/₂".

1. Cut contrasting fabric widths and lining fabric widths to the cut length from Step 3 in Fabric Calculations—Under Layer; make sure the designs in the panels match exactly.

2. If you determined in Step 2 in Fabric Calculations—Under Layer that you need more than one fabric panel to achieve the cut width, stitch fabric widths together now to achieve desired size.

3. Place contrasting fabric and lining fabric right sides together. Stitch around three sides; leave top edge open for turning (Fig. 3).

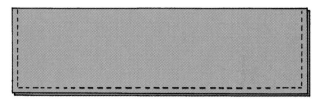

Figure 3

4. Clip bottom corners diagonally to eliminate bulk.

5. Turn the under layer right side out. Use a point turner to create sharp points. Press smooth.

Finishing the Valance

1. Cover buttons with decorator fabric (see Covering Buttons, p. 99).

2. On a large work surface, pin flaps to the under layer, right sides up. Make sure bottom edges of flaps are even with the bottom edge of the under layer.

3. Stitch through all layers across the top edge of valance.

4. Clean finish this seam by serging, overcast stitching, or enclosing the seam in bias tape.

5. Turn back the bottom edge of each flap at desired angle (Fig. 4). Press fold a hard crease. Do not fold back the flaps that cover the returns.

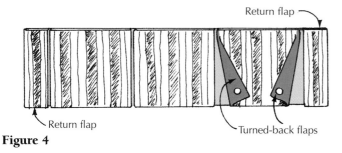

Return flap

Return flap

Turned-back flaps

Figure 4

6. Position buttons where desired and hand stitch them in place through all layers.

Installing the Valance

1. Remove mounting board from wall.

2. Secure valance to mounting board by sta-pling the top edge of the valance to the top of the board, 1/2" in from all the edges, as shown in Fig. 5. Miter corners neatly.

3. Place mounting board on angle brackets and attach the mounting board to the brackets with screws.

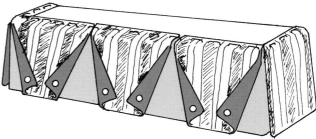

Figure 5

Cluster-Pleat Valance

This pinch-pleat valance offers a totally new look, while recalling a sentimental style. Dress up this long-time favorite with a decorative rod and the unique "clusters" of pleats. Buttons, covered with a coordinating fabric, are the perfect finishing accent.

Techniques to Know Before You Begin

Pleater hooks and pleater tape, readily available in fabric stores, are used to make the cluster-pleats in this treatment. It is a single-layered, lined valance that works beautifully with pocket panel curtains (see instructions on page 25).

Materials Needed

From the Fabric Store
- Decorator fabric (Select a medium-weight 54"-wide decorator fabric, such as damask, denim, linen, sateen, or broadcloth.)
- Lining fabric
- Sew-in "multi-pocket" pleater tape (3 times rod length)
- Pleater hooks (4-pronged) for decorative traverse rod
- Single hooks, 2 per valance
- Hook rings

- Covered button forms, $\frac{7}{8}$" diameter
- Coordinating scraps of fabric
- Thread to match decorator fabric
- Dressmaker scissors
- Water-soluble fabric marking pen
- Decorative rod, finials, and brackets (also available in hardware stores)

From the Hardware Store
- Metal measuring tape
- Carpenter's square

Fabric Calculations

Note: Mount brackets 2 to 4" above the top edge of the window frame and even with the outside edges of the window frame. Place the rod in the brackets and extend the rod slightly beyond the brackets, 1 to 3" (see Fig. 1). If you are planning to use panel curtains with this valance, you need to plan for that rod placement at this time. Use a standard flat curtain rod for this second rod, and mount it slightly below and inside the decorator rod brackets, as shown in Fig. 1. When the valance and the curtains are installed onto their respective rods, the sides and top of the panel curtains should be obscured by the valance.

Figure 1

DECORATOR FABRIC

Note: Cluster pleats are made by inserting hooks into the pockets of pleater tape. Cluster pleats are pleated in groups of three. Each cluster pleat is made with one four-pronged pleater hook; three four-pronged hooks are needed to make one group of cluster pleats. The number of groups depends upon the rod length. The pattern for creating cluster pleats in this treatment is as follows:

- *Within each pleat, one pocket is skipped between each prong*
- *No pockets are skipped between each pleat*
- *Four pockets are skipped between each group of pleats.*

1. To determine the finished width of the valance, measure the length of the mounted rod from end to end; do not include the finials.

2. Before constructing the valance, pre-pleat the pleater tape to determine the placement and spacing of pleats. Cut a length of pleater tape three times the length of the rod. Beginning 2" from one edge, insert one single hook into a tape pocket. Skip one pocket before beginning the first group of cluster pleats. To make the first pleat in the first group of cluster pleats, insert prongs into tape; skip one pocket between each prong, as shown in Fig. 2. To make the second pleat in the first group, insert the first prong into the pocket adjacent to the last pocket of the first pleat; do not skip any pockets between pleats. Make the third pleat in the first group of pleats as you did the second. Skip four pockets before beginning second group of pleats. Repeat pleating process the entire length of tape. After the last cluster, skip one pocket and insert single hook.

3. The center hook on each pleater hook is hung on the hook rings. Remove decorative rod and place as many hook rings on the rod as you have four-pronged pleater hooks, and replace the rod in brackets. Hang the tape on the rods by inserting hooks into the hook rings. Check for fit. If necessary, adjust the pleat arrangement by increasing the number of pockets between each group of cluster pleats.

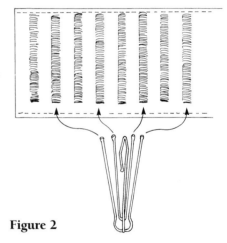

Figure 2

4. Remove the pleated tape from rod. Do not unpleat the tape yet. Trim side edges of tape 1" from single hook. On the right side of the tape, mark placement of each hook with a water-soluble pen so you can re-pleat the tape in exactly the same way when valance is finished.

5. Unpleat tape and press under $\frac{1}{2}$" on each side edge. Measure full length of tape.

6. To determine the cut width of the fabric, add 4" to the tape measurement for hem and seam allowances.

7. To determine the number of fabric widths you need to achieve the cut width, divide the cut width by the width of the fabric you are using. Round up to the next whole number.

8. To determine the finished length, measure from the bottom of the rings to the point on the window where you would like the valance to end. A good finished length is 16 to 18", but it can be any length that looks best on the window.

9. To determine the cut length, add 6½" for bottom hem and finishing allowance to the finished length.

TIP: To help you determine the perfect finished length for the valance, use newspapers to simulate the lengths. Attach a newspaper "valance" with tape. Stand back and look at the window to see if the length of the valance is in proportion to the window.

10. To calculate the total yardage of decorator fabric, multiply the cut length of the decorator fabric, from Step 9, by the number of widths you determined you need in Step 7. If you need more than one fabric width and the fabric you have selected has a repeat, multiply the repeat distance by the number of panels and add this figure to the total. The extra fabric will allow you to match the designs. Divide this number by 36, and round up to the next ¼ yard.

LINING FABRIC

1. To determine the cut width of the lining, take the cut width of the decorator fabric (Step 6 in Fabric Calculations—Decorator Fabric) and subtract 7".

2. To determine the number of fabric widths you need to achieve the cut width, divide the cut width by the width of the fabric you are using. Round up to the next whole number.

3. The cut length of the lining is 3" shorter than the cut length of the decorator fabric, found in Step 9 in Fabric Calculations—Decorator Fabric.

4. To calculate the total yardage of lining fabric, multiply the cut length of the lining fabric by the number of widths you determined you need. Divide this number by 36, and round up to the next ¼ yard.

Alternative Design

The same cluster pleating technique can be used on full-length curtains. For added pizzazz, use larger sized buttons at the base of each pleat.

Cutting Instructions

1. Straighten one end of the decorator fabric and the lining fabric using a carpenter's square.

2. Cut the decorator fabric into the appropriate cut lengths; from Step 9 in Fabric Calculations—Decorator Fabric. Make sure designs in fabric lengths match exactly.

3. Cut the lining fabric into the appropriate cut length from Step 3 in Fabric Calculations—Lining Fabric.

Construction

Note: Use ½" seam allowance unless otherwise directed.

1. Straighten one end of both fabrics with a carpenter's square.

2. If you determined in Step 7 in Fabric Calculations—Decorator Fabric that more than one fabric width is needed, sew the widths together now, and trim to attain the exact cut width, if necessary. Remember to avoid a center seam when stitching widths together. See Stitching Fabric Widths Together, page 97.

3. If you determined in Step 2 in Fabric Calculations—Lining Fabric that more than one width lining is needed, stitch the lining together now. Trim to attain the cut width, if necessary.

4. Hem the lining and decorator fabrics separately. First, hem the decorator fabric with a double 3" hem. Along the bottom edge, fold over and press 6" of fabric toward the wrong side. Tuck in the top of the hem 3" to meet the fold. Stitch or fuse the hem.

5. To hem the lining fabric, create a double 2" hem (see Step 4). Stitch or fuse hem.

6. Place decorator and lining fabrics right sides together. Pin together along one side seam. Make sure the top edge of the decorator fabric and lining fabric meet, and that the bottom edge of the lining is 1" shorter than the decorator fabric. Stitch one side seam together. Press the seam toward the lining.

7. Gently pull the lining over to meet the other side of the decorator fabric (Fig. 3). Pin this side seam together, and stitch. Press the seam toward the lining.

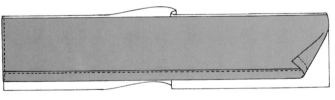

Figure 3

8. Turn valances right side out. Arrange valance so the decorator fabric "wraps" around to the lining side equally on each side, about 1½" (Fig. 4). Pin across the top edge to hold in place.

9. For a custom finish, create mitered corners (see Fig. 4). With the lining facing you, diagonally fold the bottom corners of the side hem of the decorator fabric under at a 45° angle. The point of each corner meets the side edge. Press. Hand stitch in place.

Figure 4

10. On right side of valance, mark ½" down from upper edge, using fabric marker. Pin the pleater tape along the marked line, and stitch across the top, ¼" from the edge of the tape (Fig. 5). Be careful not to stitch the pockets closed.

Figure 5

11. Fold the tape to the inside of the curtain, and press along the top edge (Fig. 6). Stitch along lower edge and both sides of tape.

Figure 6

12. To form the pleats, fold the fabric back and forth and slide the prongs or hooks into the marked pockets (Fig. 7).

13. Cover buttons with coordinating fabric (see Covering Buttons, p. 99). Hand tack button to bottom of each pleat on right side of fabric.

Installing and "Dressing" the Valance

1. Place pleated panels on rod; insert hooks into rings.

Figure 7

2. Arrange pleats evenly on rod.

Lined Rod Pocket Panel Curtains

Note: This treatment features a single lined layer. These simple panel curtains can be used with most of the valances in this chapter.

Fabric Calculations

1. Measure the length of the rod plus the returns (the end projections that extend from the wall).

2. To determine the finished width, multiply by 2½ or 3, depending on fullness desired.

3. To determine the cut width, add 12" to the finished width for the side hems.

4. To determine number of fabric widths you need, divide the cut width by the width of the fabric you are using. Round up to the next whole number.

5. To determine the finished length, measure from the top of the rod to where you would like the curtains to end.

6. To determine the cut length, add 11" to the finished width, for rod pocket and hem allowances.

7. To calculate the total yardage of decorator fabric, multiply the cut length by the number of widths you determined you need in Step 4. (If you need more than one fabric width and the fabric you have selected has a repeat, multiply the repeat distance by the number of panels and add this figure to the total. The extra fabric will allow you to match the designs.) Divide this number by 36, and round up to the next ¼ yard.

8. You will need the same number of lining fabric widths as the number of fabric widths from Step 4.

9. To calculate the total yardage of lining fabric, multiply the cut length by the number of widths you need. Divide this number by 36, and round up to the next ¼ yard.

Construction

1. Straighten one end of both fabrics using a carpenter's square.

2. Cut decorator fabric to the cut length from Step 6 in Fabric Calculations; make sure the designs in the fabric match exactly.

3. Cut lining to the cut length from Step 8 in Fabric Calculations.

4. If you determined that you need more than one fabric width to achieve the cut widths of the layers, sew all the fabric widths together now, and trim to achieve the exact cut width measurement, if necessary. Remember to avoid a center seam when stitching widths together. See Stitching Fabric Widths Together, page 97.

5. Repeat Step 4 with lining. Trim 6" from one selvage and 3" from the bottom edge.

6. Hem the lining and decorator fabric separately. Create a double 4" hem at the bottom of the decorator fabric. Along the bottom edges fold over and press 8" of fabric toward the wrong side. Next, tuck in the top of the hem 4" to meet the fold. Stitch or fuse hem.

7. To hem the lining fabric, create a double 3" hem (see Step 6). Stitch or fuse hem.

8. Center wrong side of lining against the wrong side of decorator fabric; match upper edges.

9. Finish each side of the panel by creating a double 1½" hem. At the side of each panel, fold over and press 3" of fabric toward the lining. Next, tuck in the edge of the hem 1½" to meet the fold, enclosing the lining in the process. Stitch or fuse hem. For a professional finish, blind stitch the hem.

10. To create the rod pocket, press top edge of both layers down ½", toward lining. Fold again 1½", pin, and stitch close to first fold line.

Installing and "Dressing" the Valance

1. Slip panels on rod through rod pockets.

2. Arrange fabric evenly on rod.

Tabbed Roman Shade

The addition of tabs to a Roman shade transforms this treatment into an "uptown" version of a traditional favorite. It also takes advantage of some of the wonderful decorative hardware that's available.

The working mechanisms of this shade are mounted on a wooden board and hidden behind the top edge of the shade. The decorative rod and finials serve only a decorative purpose.

Installing the Hardware

Note: The working mechanism of the shade is attached to a mounting board. The rod for the tabs is purely decorative. Select a rod with a short bracket that protrudes from the wall only far enough to allow the shade to lie against the wall.

1. Measure and mount the rod and brackets carefully; they are integral to the finished treatment. Determine the length of the mounting board (the finished width of the shade). If the window has a frame, measure the width from outside frame edge to outside frame edge, and add 1". If the window has a sill or a trim that protrudes from the frame, measure the width at that sill or trim, and add 1". If the window does not have a frame, measure the window opening, and add 2".

2. Prepare the mounting board by either painting it to match the wall color or by covering the board with decorator fabric. Install the board above the window like a shelf. Secure angle brackets to the wall, and rest mounting board on them. Allow at least 1" clearance between the bottom of the board and the top of the frame for the screw eyes. Note: Do not yet permanently attach the board to the brackets, as you will need it later when attaching the shade.

3. Install the rod above the board (Fig. 1).

The distance between the rod and the mounting board will determine the length of the tabs. The top edge of the shade should be slightly *above* the top edge of the mounting board. Keep in mind that the tabs are even with the outside edges of the shade and the brackets should not interfere with tab placement.

Figure 1

Fabric Calculations

1. The cut width of the shade is equal to the length of the mounting board, from Step 1 in Installing the Hardware, plus 6".

2. To determine the finished length of the window treatment, measure from the top edge of the mounting board to either the top of the window sill or the bottom of the apron—wherever you would like your shade to end. To determine the cut length, add 5" for top and bottom finishing allowances.

3. To determine the number of fabric widths you need to achieve the cut width, divide the cut width by the width of the fabric you are using. Round up to the next whole number.

4. To determine the total yardage, first multiply the number of widths you need by the cut length of the fabric from Step 2. (If you need more than one fabric panel and the fabric you have selected has a repeat, multiply the repeat distance by the number of panels and add this figure to the total. The extra fabric will allow you to match the designs.) Divide this number by 36 and round up to the next 1/4 yard. Add 1/2 additional yardage for tabs. If you plan to cover the mounting board with decorator fabric, be sure to include the amount you will need to do this is in the total yardage.

5. To determine the total yardage of lining fabric, first multiply the cut length by the number of panels needed. Divide this number by 36 and round up to the next 1/4 yard.

6. To determine the length of the tabs, drape a string over the rod and pin it together where you plan to have the top edge of the shade (Fig. 2). Note: The top edge of the shade should be slightly above the top edge of the mounting board. Mark the string before removing it from the rod and measure the distance between the marks. To achieve cut length, add 1 1/2".

7. The finished width of the tab is 5"; the cut

Materials Needed

From the Fabric Store
- Decorative rod, finials, and brackets (also available in hardware stores)
- Decorator fabric for shade (Select a medium-weight 54"-wide decorator fabric, such as chintz, damask, denim, lightweight canvas, moiré, polished cotton, sateen, or broadcloth.)
- Lining fabric
- Thread to match both decorator and lining fabrics
- Stitch-in ring tape
- Thread to match ring tape
- Stitch-in hook-and-loop tape
- Nylon cord
- Cord cleat
- Cord pulls (one for each shade)

- Screw eyes (one for each row of cording)
- Fabric marking pen or pencil
- Zipper foot
- Dressmaker scissors

From the Hardware Store
- 1 × 2" wood mounting board
- Carpenter's square
- Angle brackets (at least 2, and then 1 for every 36" of finished width)
- Weight bar (wooden dowel or café rod, 1" shorter than finished width of shade)
- Screws, 2" long (2–4 for every angle bracket)
- *Optional:* Heavy-duty staple gun with 5/8" staples

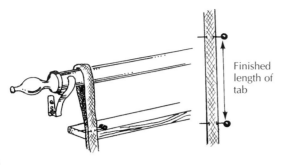

Figure 2

width is 11". Cut an odd number of tabs to fit the width of your shade. The space between the tabs is entirely up to you.

Construction

Note: All seam allowances are ¹/₂" unless otherwise noted.

SHADE

1. Use a carpenter's square to straighten one end of the decorator fabric and the lining fabric.

2. Cut fabric and lining to the cut length determined in Step 2 in Fabric Calculations.

3. Trim lining widths *only* to the *finished* length (from Step 2 in Fabric Calculations) and *finished* width (from Step 1 in Installing the Hardware).

4. If you determined in Step 3 in Fabric Calculations that you need more than one width to achieve the cut width, sew the decorator fabric widths together and the lining fabric widths together now. Trim if necessary. Remember to avoid a center seam when stitching widths together. See Stitching Fabric Widths Together, page 97.

5. Cut ring tape into lengths equal to the finished length of the fabric, from Step 2 in Fabric Calculations.

6. To form side hems, lay the decorator fabric right side down on a large work surface. At the side of each panel, fold over and press 3" of fabric toward the lining. Next, tuck in the edge of the hem 1¹/₂" to meet the fold (Fig. 3). Press.

7. At the bottom of each panel, fold over and press 4" of fabric toward the wrong side. Next, tuck in the top of the hem 2" to meet the fold. Press.

8. Fold the top edge over and press ³/₄"

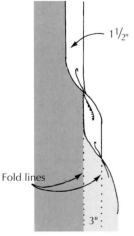

Fold lines

Figure 3

toward the wrong side (Fig. 4).

9. Place the lining on the wrong side of the shade; tuck raw edges of lining under the hem allowances (Fig. 5). Pin in place.

10. Still working from the wrong side, measure the distance between inside edges of side hems. Divide this measurement into equal sections about 8" to 10" apart. Mark division points with fabric pencil (Fig. 6).

11. Place ring tape over marked lines and center over folded side hem edges. Place bottom ring next to the edge of bottom hem; extend tape into hem allowance about 1¹/₂". Remove any rings that may end up in the bottom hem. Run the tape vertically and extend under the ³/₄" fold along top edge, as shown (Fig. 7). Repeat with all rows of tape. Note: All rings must line up horizontally across the shade.

12. Thread the sewing machine by placing the thread that matches the decorator fabric in the bobbin and the thread that matches the tape in the top position. Using a

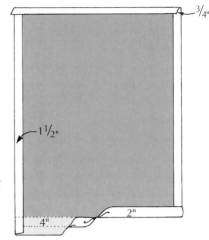

Figure 4

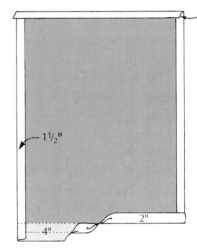

Figure 5

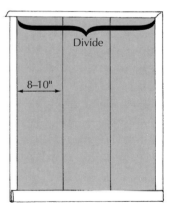

Figure 6

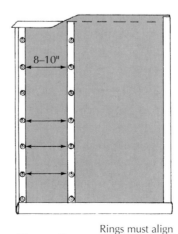

Figure 7   Rings must align horizontally

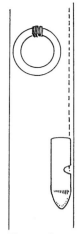

Figure 8

zipper foot, stitch tape in place along edges (Fig. 8).

13. Now thread the machine so both top and bobbin thread match the decorator fabric. Refold the bottom hem and stitch through all layers.

TIP: To eliminate the stitching lines on the outside of the Roman shade, you can use iron-on ring tape or individual rings. To use iron-on tape, place fusible tape directly on each planned ring tape line. (Iron-on ring tape requires that you secure the lining to decorator fabric with fusible tape.) If you use individual rings, the position for each ring must be exact and each ring must line up vertically and horizontally. Hand or machine stitch rings in place through all layers.

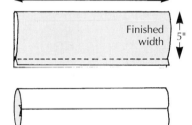

Finished length of tab plus 1½"

Finished width 5"

Figure 9

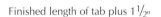

Stitch ¾" from top edge along fold line.

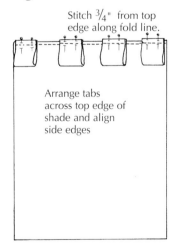

Arrange tabs across top edge of shade and align side edges

Figure 10

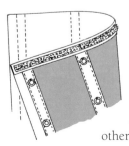

Figure 11

TABS

1. To make each tab, fold strip in half lengthwise with right sides together. Stitch along long edge. Press seam open lightly before turning. Turn tabs right side out. Center seam in the back of each tab and press flat (Fig. 9).

2. Lay shade right side up on large work surface. Unfold the top edge of the shade, and determine the placement of each tab. The first and last tab should be even with each side edge. The remaining tabs should be evenly spaced between these two. Fold tab in half so raw edges are even and seam is on inside. Pin tabs in place to right side of shade; align raw edges of tabs and shade (Fig 10).

3. Stitch through all layers directly over the ¾" fold line. Clean finish the raw edges by serging or overcasting. Refold on fold line, so that tabs are loop end up.

4. Stitch the sew-on loop side of hook-and-loop tape to the right side along the top folded edge (Fig. 11). One edge of the tape should be even with the ¾" fold line and the other edge within the seam allowance.

Rigging the Shade

1. Remove the board from wall. Staple hook side of fastener tape to one long narrow edge of board (Fig. 12). Attach the shade to the mounting board by pressing the hook and loop tape together securely.

Staple hook side of tape to board

Figure 12

2. Place shade and board wrong side up on work surface. Insert screw eyes into the bottom of the board above each row of rings.

3. Determine from what side the shade will be raised and lowered. Beginning on the opposite side, cut a length of nylon cord for each row of rings. Note: Each cord will be a different length. Each cord should be long enough to form a knot at the bottom-most ring, go up through the row of rings, across the top of the shade, and half way down the other side.

4. For each row of ring tape, secure cording to bottom ring by tying a square knot; reinforce with a bit of glue. Thread cording up through all rings in each row, then across the width of the shade through screw eyes (Fig. 13). Repeat for every row of rings. When you have finished threading and all cords are along one side, tie them together with a knot in the end. Attach a cord pull.

Estimating Tape and Cord Yardage

1. Determine the number of rows of rings. Divide the finished width by 8 to 10", whatever divides evenly. (This is the distance between strips of ring tape on your shade.) Add 2, for the tapes on each side.

2. Estimate the ring tape yardage. Multiply the number of rows of rings by the cut length of the fabric. Divide by 36.

3. Estimate the nylon cord yardage. Multiply the number of rows of rings by 2. Multiply the number of rows of rings by the width of the shade. Add these two numbers together. Divide by 36.

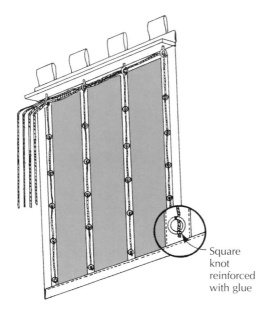

Square knot reinforced with glue

Figure 13

5. Adjust the tension of each cord so when the cords are pulled, the shade will raise up in even horizontal folds. When you are satisfied with the way the shade raises and lowers, knot the cords together just below the outermost screw eye. Tie several more knots into the cording at even increments so you can secure the shade to the awning cleat at different levels

TIP: It's a good idea to "train" your Roman Shade. Before hanging, draw the shade up to the board and secure the cords. Arrange the folds so they are smooth and horizontal across the shade. Use a few scraps of fabric to tie the folds in place. Leave the shade in place for several days before mounting permanently.

Installing the Shade

1. Install cord cleat on the side of the window from which the shade will be raised and lowered, about halfway down the window.

2. Place mounting board at window. You may need a friend to help to move the shade to the window so the cords don't get tangled.

3. Remove the rod from the brackets and insert rod through tabs. Replace rod in brackets.

4. Unfurl the shade. Insert weight bar into opening in bottom hem (Fig. 14). Hand stitch opening closed to secure bar in place.

Alternative Design

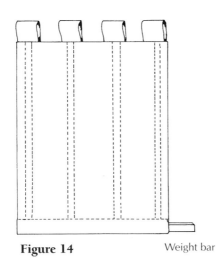

Figure 14   Weight bar

To create this great bordered look, use one fabric for the center section of the shade and one fabric for the border. Treat this unit as one throughout the construction process. Instead of adding wide fabric tabs, hand sew decorative rings to the top edge of the shade.

Cord-and-Eyelet Tab Curtain

Easy, breezy window treatments are the newest trend in decorating. And no wonder! Besides being super simple to make, this design fits any decor: elegant, traditional, or contemporary.

Techniques to Know Before You Begin

Eyelets are installed across the top edge of this window treatment. Decorative cording is laced through the eyelets and over the top edge to act as the "tabs." These unlined curtains are hemmed on all sides.

Materials Needed

From the Fabric Store
- Decorator fabric (Select a medium-weight 54"-wide decorator fabric such as damask, denim, linen, sateen, or broadcloth. Since this treatment is unlined, use a fabric that looks the same on the back and front.)
- Thread to match decorator fabric
- Eyelets, 7 per 54" panel
- Decorative cording, 4 yards (make sure cording fits hole in eyelet)

- Decorative rod, finials, and brackets (also available at department and hardware stores)
- Fabric marking pen or pencil
- *Optional:* Paper-backed fusible tape for hems
- *Optional:* Decorative holdbacks and finials
- *Optional:* Eyelet pliers (highly recommended!)

From the Hardware Store
- Carpenter's square

Fabric Calculations

Note: These instructions will result in panels that are each approximately 48" wide. This size is suitable for windows up to 60" wide at 1½ times fullness. If your window is wider than 60", you must add the appropriate number of fabric panels to achieve the width and re-calculate the yardage. To calculate cording for a larger window, multiply the finished width of each panel by 1.5, and divide by 36. For help, see Yardage Calculations, page 94.

1. Mount the hardware 2 to 4" above the top edge of the window frame and 1 to 4" out from each side edge of the window frame (Fig. 1). This rod position will minimize light leaks, and the heading will not show from the outside.

2. To determine the cut length of each fabric, measure from the top edge of the window frame to the floor, and add 13" for top and bottom hem allowances. Note: If you plan to puddle this treatment, add 7 to 12" to the cut length measurement.

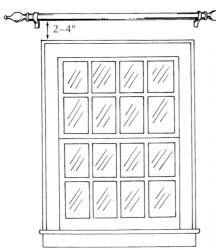

Figure 1

3. To determine the total yardage, first multiply the cut length by 2 for the second curtain panel. (If the fabric has a repeat, multiply the repeat distance by 2 and add this figure to

the total.) Divide this number by 36 and round number up to next ¼ yard.

Construction

Note: Use ½" seam allowance unless otherwise directed.

1. Use a carpenter's square to straighten one end of the decorator fabric. Cut fabric panels to their cut length.

2. Cut decorator fabric to the cut length in Step 2 in Fabric Calculations; make sure designs in fabric lengths match exactly.

3. Hem the bottom of each panel with a double 4" hem. Fold over and press 8" of fabric toward the wrong side. Next, tuck in the top of the hem 4" to meet the fold. Stitch or fuse hem. Note: If you are planning to puddle the hem, just create a double ½" hem—or leave the hem unfinished! See the tip on Puddled Hems, page 35.

4. For side hems, trim off selvages. Then create a double 2" hem (see Step 3). Stitch or fuse hem; stop stitching 4" from the top edge.

5. To finish top edge, fold over and press 4" toward the wrong side. Then tuck under 2" to meet the fold to create a double 2" hem (see Step 2). Press. Open out hem and trim away *one layer only* of the top section (see Figs. 2 and 3). This will eliminate some bulk when applying eyelets in the corners. For a professional finish, form a mitered corner. Fold the corner at a 45° angle to meet the fold line, and then refold top hem into a double 2" hem (Fig. 3). Stitch or fuse hem.

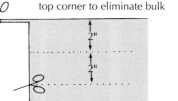

Trim away one layer only of the top corner to eliminate bulk

Figure 2

6. Determine the placement of eyelets along top edge of each panel. All eyelets should be approximately ½" down from the top. The first and last eyelet should be at each top corner approximately ½" in from the side

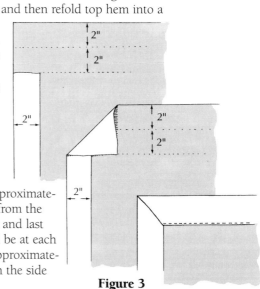

Figure 3

edge. The remaining eyelets should be spaced approximately 6 to 8" apart (Fig. 4). Mark eyelet position on wrong side of fabric by tracing around inside opening of eyelet with a fabric marking pen or pencil.

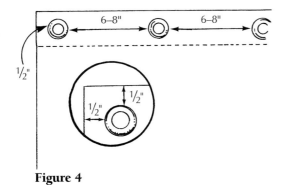

Figure 4

7. Attach eyelets where marked; follow manufacturer's instructions. A pair of eyelet pliers makes this job easier!

8. Cut cording in half. To lace cording through eyelets, make a large single knot at one end of the cord and wrap masking tape around other end so that it acts as a needle. Begin at outside corner of each panel. Insert taped end through eyelet from front to back; pull cord until knot is against eyelet, on the right side of fabric. Bring the cording over the top edge to the front and insert through the next eyelet (Fig. 5). Continue in this manner until all eyelets are used. When all eyelets are laced, make a large single knot on end to secure.

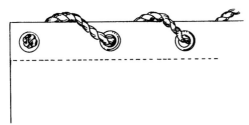

Figure 5

Installing and "Dressing" the Curtain

1. Insert rod through cording and place rods in brackets.

2. Make sure cording is evenly distributed across the top edge. The top of the curtain should be straight. Arrange fabric into folds as desired.

3. *Optional:* Place one or both sides of curtain into holdbacks.

❧ "Puddling" is a real time-saver when you are making your own curtains. You don't even have to finish the hem if you don't want to — just leave the edges unfinished; they'll be hidden in the luxurious folds that puddling creates. To puddle a window treatment, gather the bottom edge and secure it with a rubber band or by tying it with cord. Tuck the raw edges inside the "pocket" that forms and place on floor. Arrange fabric on floor as desired.

Contrasting-
Buttonhole Tab Curtain

Choose an upbeat coordinating fabric for the buttonholes that top off this uniquely styled window covering. I used denim for the main part of the curtain, but you could use nearly any type of fabric.

The buttonholed cuff on this treatment is created separately from the main portion of the curtain and then attached to it. The rod is woven through the buttonholes at the top of each panel. The curtains are not lined.

Techniques to Know Before You Begin

Materials Needed

From the Fabric Store
- Decorator fabric for main portion of curtain (Select a medium-weight 54"-wide fabric, such as damask, denim, linen, sateen, or broadcloth. Since this treatment is unlined, use a fabric that looks the same on the front and back.)
- 7/8 yard of contrasting fabric for the heading (Use a fabric the same weight and width as your main fabric.)
- 1/4 yard of tightly woven fabric for buttonhole trim

- Thread to match decorator fabric
- Non-permanent fabric marking pen or pencil
- Point turner
- Dressmaker scissors
- Sharp embroidery scissors
- Template plastic or tissue paper
- Decorative rod, finials, and brackets (also available in hardware and department stores)
- *Optional:* Decorative hold-backs

From the Hardware Store
- Carpenter's square

Fabric Calculations

Note: These instructions will result in panels that are each 48" wide. This size is suitable for windows up to 60" wide at 1½ times fullness. If your window is wider than 60", you must add the appropriate number of fabric widths to achieve the width and re-calculate the yardage. For help, see Yardage Calculations, page 94.

Figure 1

1. Mount the hardware 3" above the top edge of the window frame and even with each outside edge of the window frame (Fig. 1). Note: The top edge of curtain will extend 2¼" above the rod.

2. To determine the cut length of the bottom portion of the curtain, measure from the top edge of the window frame to the floor and add 6¾" for finishing allowance.

3. To determine the total yardage of main fabric, first multiply the cut length by 2 for the second curtain panel. (If the fabric has a repeat, multiply the repeat distance by 2 and add this figure to the total.) Divide this number by 36 and round number up to next ¼ yard.

Cutting Instructions

1. Straighten one end of the main fabric by using a carpenter's square.

2. Cut the fabric widths to the cut length determined in Step 2 in Fabric Calculations; make sure designs in fabric lengths match exactly.

3. From the heading fabric, cut two strips, each 15" wide by 54" (the width of the fabric).

4. Trace the buttonhole pattern (below) onto template plastic or tissue paper and cut the pattern out. Cut 16 buttonhole shapes from the buttonhole trim fabric. Be sure to transfer the stitching lines onto the wrong side of the fabric.

Construction

Note: Use ½" seam allowance unless otherwise directed.

1. At the bottom of each panel, create a double 4" hem. Fold over and press 8" of fabric toward the wrong side. Next, tuck in the top of the hem 4" to meet the fold. Stitch or fuse hem.

2. Make side hems. First, trim off all selvages. Then create a double 2" hem by folding over and pressing 4" of fabric toward the wrong side. Next, tuck in the edge of the hem 2" to

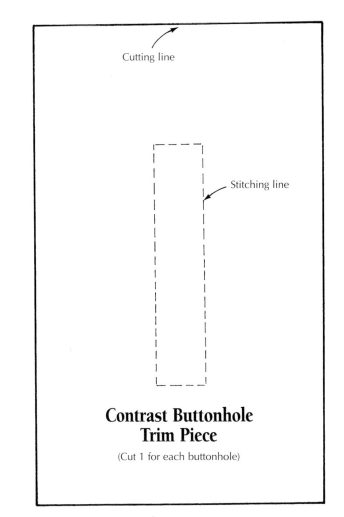

Cutting line

Stitching line

Contrast Buttonhole Trim Piece

(Cut 1 for each buttonhole)

meet the fold. Stitch or fuse hem. *Measure the finished width of the panel and note it.*

3. Make the heading. Fold the strip in half lengthwise with right sides together so it measures 7½ by 54". Press lightly. Along one long edge, fold ½" toward the wrong side and press (Fig. 2). Now trim and stitch the heading so that it equals the finished width of the panel. Trim the corners diagonally to eliminate bulk. Turn heading right side out. Use a point turner to gently push the fabric out from the inside to create sharp corners. Press flat.

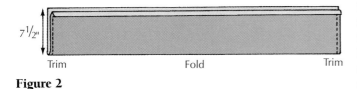

Figure 2

4. The side with the *unfolded* edge is the *back side* of the heading. Working on the back side, use a non-permanent pen or pencil to mark the placement of the buttonholes. Mark 1" down from the top edge along the entire width of the heading. Make a vertical mark 1½" in from each side edge. Divide the remaining area into seven sections, each approximately 6" apart, and mark. Draw a vertical line the entire length of the heading at each mark (Fig. 3).

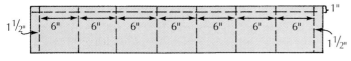

Figure 3

5. Center buttonhole trim (right side down) over each guide line. Be sure the top edge of trim is 1" from top edge of the heading. Stitch around the center area of the trim on the stitching line (Fig. 4).

6. Use embroidery scissors to carefully cut through the opening and trim away fabric that is within the smaller rectangle very close to the stitching line. Carefully clip to the corner; make sure you do not cut the stitching line.

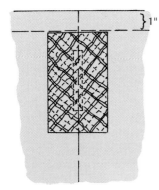

Figure 4

7. Bring the trim through the hole to the front of the heading and press smooth. Press all edges of buttonhole trim under ½" toward wrong side. Pin trim in place. Carefully topstitch around the buttonhole and outside edges of buttonhole trim (Fig. 5).

8. Attach the heading to the panel. Place the wrong side of the curtain to the back side of the heading, with the fold of the heading facing down. Pin the top edge of the panel to the unfolded edge of the heading. The heading should fit the width of the panel exactly. Stitch through all layers. Be careful not to catch any of the front side of the heading in the seam. Press the seam down toward the heading (Fig. 6).

9. Turn entire curtain over so the right side is facing you. Bring the folded edge of the heading down so it is even with the stitched seam. Top stitch heading in place. The seam that originally attached the heading to the curtain is now enclosed in the heading (Fig. 7).

Installing and "Dressing" the Curtain

1. Weave the rod through buttonholes and place rod in bracket. Extend the rod slightly beyond the brackets, 1 to 3". Arrange the fabric into folds as desired.

2. If you like, place one or both sides of curtain in holdbacks.

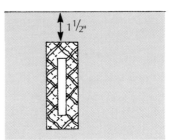

Figure 5

Figure 6

Figure 7

Shaped Tab Curtain

I just love the shape of these tabs, don't you? And the covered buttons provide the perfect custom finish. Use two coordinating fabrics as I did to create this great look. If you're nervous about making buttonholes, don't worry. These buttonholes are just an illusion!

Techniques to Know Before You Begin

The shaped tabs on this treatment are created with a pattern you trace right from this book. You can use two coordinating fabrics, or just one for a more uniform look. The treatment can be lined or unlined.

Materials Needed

From the Fabric Store
- Decorator fabric (Select a medium-weight 54"-wide fabric, such as damask, denim, linen, sateen, or broadcloth. If you choose not to line the curtain for a more casual look, use a fabric that looks the same on the front and back.)
- ½ yard coordinating fabric for 8 tabs (4 per panel)
- 8 button cover sets, ⅞" diameter

- Thread to match decorator fabric
- Non-permanent fabric marking pen or pencil
- Point turner
- Dressmaker scissors
- Template plastic or tissue paper
- Decorative rod, finials, and brackets (also available in hardware and department stores)
- *Optional:* Decorative holdbacks

From the Hardware Store
- Carpenter's square

Fabric Calculations

Note: These instructions will result in panels that are each 48" wide. This size is suitable for windows up to 60" wide at 1½ times fullness. If your window is wider than 60", you must add the appropriate number of fabric widths to achieve the width and re-calculate the yardage. For help, see Yardage Calculations, page 94.

1. Mount the hardware 3" above the top edge of the window frame and 1 to 4" out from each side edge of the window frame (Fig. 1).

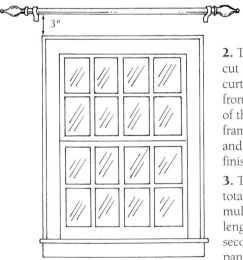

Figure 1

2. To determine the cut length of the curtain, measure from the top edge of the window frame to the floor and add 8½" for finishing allowance.

3. To determine the total yardage, first multiply the cut length by 2 for the second curtain panel. (If the fabric has a repeat, multiply the repeat distance by 2 and add this figure to the total.) Add 9" for facing. Divide this number by 36 and round number up to next ¼ yard.

Cutting Instructions

1. Straighten one end of the fabric by using a carpenter's square

2. Cut the fabric to the cut length determined in Step 2 in Fabric Calculations.

3. From the extra fabric, cut two facing strips, each 3" wide by 54"—the width of fabric.

4. Trace the tab pattern on page 41 onto template plastic or tissue paper and cut the pattern out. From the coordinating fabric, cut 16 tab shapes.

Construction

Note: Use ½" seam allowance unless indicated otherwise.

1. At the bottom of each panel, create a double 4" hem. Fold over and press 8" of fabric toward the wrong side. Next, tuck in the top of the hem 4" to meet the fold. Stitch or fuse hem.

2. Make side hems. First, trim off all selvages. Then create a double 2" hem by folding over and pressing 4" of fabric toward the wrong side. Next, tuck in the edge of the hem 2" to meet the fold. Stitch or fuse hem. Measure the finished width of the panel and note it.

3. To make each tab, place two tab shapes right sides together. Stitch as shown in Fig. 2, using ¼" seam allowance. Carefully cut notches from curved edge of seam allowance—be careful not to cut through stitching line. Turn tabs right side out; use a point turner to make sure the curve is smooth. Press flat.

¼" seam allowance

Figure 2

4. Along the top edge of each panel, determine the placement of each tab; the first and last tab should be as close to each side edge as possible—the tips may have to extend slightly from the edge of the curtain for a smooth corner. The remaining tabs should be evenly spaced approximately 5½" apart (Fig. 3). Pin tabs in place on right side of curtain; align raw edges of tabs and curtain.

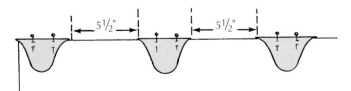

Figure 3

5. Now prepare facing strips so that they equal the finished width of the panel. Trim the facing strip so it is 1" longer than the finished width of the curtain panel.

6. Press under ½" along one of the *long* edges toward wrong side. Fold and press each side under ½" toward wrong side.

7. With right sides together, pin the unfolded edge of the facing to the upper edge of curtain; sandwich tabs between the two layers. The edge of the facing should be even with the edge of the curtain. Stitch along upper edge (Fig. 4). Grade seam allowances. Turn facing to wrong side of curtain and press. Stitch facing to curtain along bottom edge and side edges (Fig. 5).

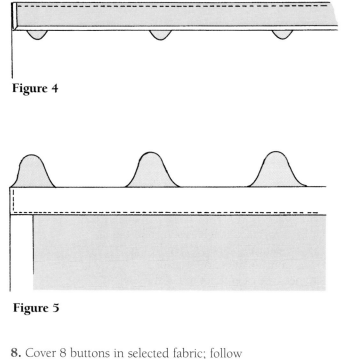

Figure 4

Figure 5

8. Cover 8 buttons in selected fabric; follow manufacturer's instructions.

9. Fold each tab over so the curved tip of the tab extends 1½" below the top edge of the curtain. Tack tabs in place at the button placement. Center covered button on tab and secure button by stitching through all layers of fabric (Fig. 6).

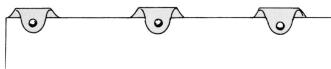

Figure 6

Installing and "Dressing" the Curtain.

1. Insert rod through tabs and place rod in bracket. Extend the rod slightly beyond the brackets, 1 to 3". Arrange the fabric into folds as desired.

2. *Optional:* Place one or both sides of curtain in a holdback.

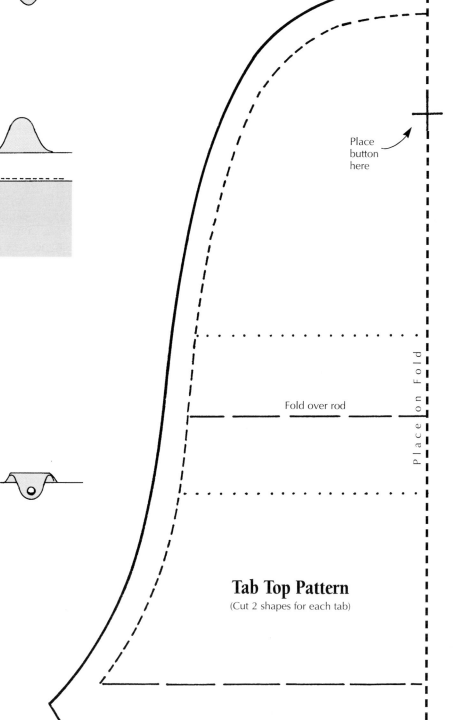

Place button here

Place on Fold

Fold over rod

Tab Top Pattern
(Cut 2 shapes for each tab)

Gathered Tab Curtain

This treatment would look great in any room. The tabs resemble neckties, but they are wider so they can be gathered and held in place by—are you ready for this—napkin rings! I painted these to match the rod for a super finishing touch. If you want, personalize the napkin rings by adding trims, fabric, or ribbons to their edges.

Strips of fabrics are used for ties in this lined treatment. These ties can be cut on the straight of grain or on the bias.

Techniques to Know Before You Begin

Materials Needed

From the Fabric Store

- Decorator fabric (Select a medium-weight 54"-wide fabric, such as damask, denim, linen, sateen, or broadcloth.)
- 2½ yards coordinating fabric for tabs to make 5 tabs per panel (The bias-cut tabs shown in the photo require more yardage. Take the tab pattern to the fabric store to determine your yardage and ensure the bias-cut tabs are identical.)
- Lining fabric, 54" wide

- Napkin rings, one for each tab
- Thread to match decorator fabric
- Non-permanent fabric marking pen or pencil
- Point turner
- Dressmaker scissors
- Decorative rod, 1⅜" diameter, finials, and brackets (also available in hardware and department stores)

From the Hardware Store

- Carpenter's square

Fabric Calculations

Note: These instructions will result in panels that are each 48" wide. This size is suitable for windows up to 60" wide at 1½ times fullness. If your window is wider than 60", you must add the appropriate number of fabric widths to achieve the width and re-calculate the yardage. For help, see Yardage Calculations, page 94.

1. Mount the hardware 2 to 4" above the top edge of the window frame and 1 to 2" out from each side edge of the window frame (Fig. 1).

Figure 1

2. Determine the cut length of the curtain and lining. Measure from the top edge of the window frame to the floor and add 8½" for finishing allowance.

3. To determine the total yardage of decorator fabric and lining fabric, first multiply the cut length by 2 for the second curtain panel. (If the fabric has a repeat, multiply the repeat distance by 2 and add this figure to the total.) Divide this number by 36 and round number up to next ¼ yard.

Cutting Instructions

1. Use a carpenter's square to straighten one end of both fabrics.

2. Cut the decorator fabric and lining fabric to the cut length determined in Step 2 in Fabric Calculations; make sure designs in fabric lengths match exactly. Trim each *lining* panel 6" along one selvage and 3" along the bottom.

3. Cut out the tabs. From coordinating fabric cut 10 *lengthwise* strips, each 13 by 30". (Lengthwise means cut parallel to selvage.)

4. To form the diagonal ends of ties, fold each strip in half lengthwise with right sides together. Measure and mark a 45° diagonal line along one end. Cut along these lines and discard the triangles (Fig. 2).

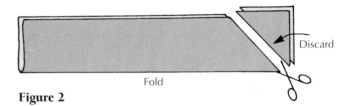

Discard

Fold

Figure 2

Construction

Note: Use ½" seam allowance unless indicated otherwise.

1. Make tabs. Begin at folded edge and stitch across diagonal line and long edge. Trim away corner to reduce bulk (Fig. 3). Turn tabs right side out. Use a point turner to gently push fabric out from the inside and create sharp points. Press flat.

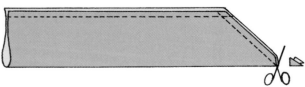

Figure 3

2. Finger pleat the top edge of the tab—make one or two folds in the fabric—so it now measures 2" (Fig. 4). Pin to hold shape.

3. Hem the decorator and lining panels separately. At the bottom of each decorator panel, create a double 4" hem. First, fold over and

Figure 4

press 8" of fabric toward the wrong side. Next, tuck in the top of the hem 4" to meet the fold. Stitch or fuse hem. To hem the lining fabric, create a double 3" hem. First, fold over and press 6" of fabric toward the wrong side. Next, tuck in the top of the hem 3" to meet the fold. Stitch or fuse hem.

4. Place decorator fabric and lining right sides together. Pin together along one side seam. Make sure the top edges of the decorator fabric and lining fabric are even, and that the bottom edge of the lining is 1" shorter than the decorator fabric. Stitch one side seam together (Fig. 5). Press the seam toward the lining.

5. Gently pull the lining over to meet the other side of the decorator fabric. Pin this side seam together, and stitch. Press the seam toward the lining.

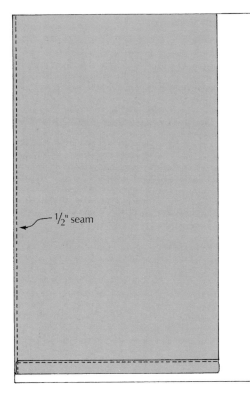

Figure 5

6. With the decorator fabric and lining fabric still right sides together, place the curtain on a large surface. Arrange the curtain so the decorator fabric "wraps" around to the lining side equally on each side, about 1½". Pin across the top edge to hold in place.

7. Determine the placement of each tab along the top edge of each panel. The first and last tab should be as close to each side as possible; the remaining tabs evenly spaced between these two.

8. Insert the tabs between the lining and the decorator panels with the pointed end of the tab toward the bottom hem. Double-check that the diagonal edges of the tabs are going in the same direction! Be sure the raw edges of the tabs, decorator fabric, and lining fabric are even along the top edge. Stitch through all layers across the top edge (Fig. 6). Clip corners diagonally to eliminate bulk.

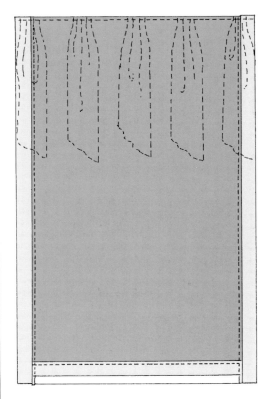

Figure 6

9. Turn curtains right sides out. Arrange the curtain so the decorator fabric "wraps" around to the back equally on each side from the top of the curtain to the bottom hem. Press fabric smooth.

Shading Legend

	Primary Fabric Right Side
	Primary Fabric Wrong Side
	Lining for Primary Fabric
	Contrasting Fabric Right Side
	Contrasting Fabric Wrong Side

10. For a custom hem finish, create mitered corners at the bottom of the decorator panels. With wrong side facing you, diagonally fold *under*—at a 45° angle—the bottom corner of the side hem until the point of each corner meets the side edge *inside the side hem*. Press. Hand stitch in place (Fig. 7).

2. Gather the tab together along the top edge of the curtain. Insert the fold of the tab through the napkin ring (Fig 9). If napkin ring slips off the tab, pin the tab together inconspicuously with a straight pin.

3. Insert the rod through the tabs and place the rod in the bracket.

4. Arrange fabric into folds as desired and distribute gathers evenly at each tab.

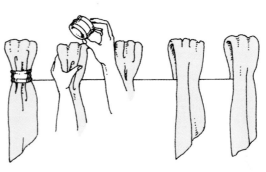

Figure 9

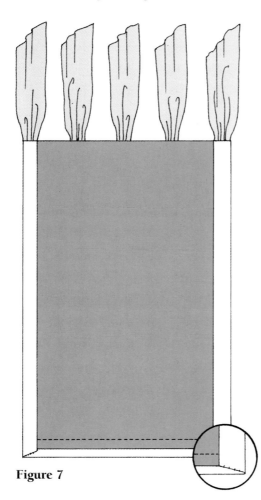

Figure 7

Installing and "Dressing" the Curtain

1. Place curtain on large flat surface, right side up. Fold the tabs over toward the front of the curtain. Each tab should extend 3" above the top edge of the curtain (Fig. 8).

Alternative Design

This window treatment is perfect for wide windows! Simply make an extra curtain in the same proportions as described in the instructions and hang it in the middle of the window.

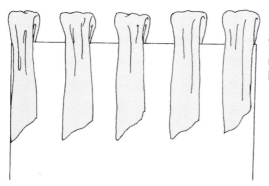

Figure 8

Pinch-Pleat Draperies and Swag Scarf

You'll be pleasantly surprised at how easy these pinch pleats are to construct. The scarf is draped elegantly over the treatment for a dramatic effect and is cleverly self-lined on each end so that the folds show only the wonderful fabric.

This lined drapery utilizes pleater tape to ease the pleating process. Use fabric of any width to create the scarf, which is mostly unlined.

Techniques to Know Before You Begin

Fabric Calculations—Draperies

1. Mount the hardware 2 to 4" above the top edge of the window frame and 1 to 4" out from each side edge of the window frame (Fig. 1).

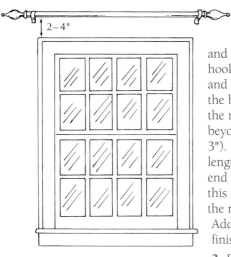

Figure 1

2. Determine the cut width of the decorator and lining fabric. Place hook rings on the rod and place the rod in the brackets. Extend the rod slightly beyond brackets (1 to 3"). Measure the length of the rod from end to end. Multiply this number by 2½ for the necessary fullness. Add 8" to the total for finishing allowance.

3. Determine the number of fabric widths you need. Divide the cut width by the width of fabric you are using. Round up to the next whole number.

4. Determine the cut length of the decorator fabric. Measure from the bottom of the rings to the desired finished length. The two best finished lengths are floor-length or to the bottom of the apron. Add 8½" to the total for finishing allowance.

5. Determine the yardage. Multiply the cut length by the number of widths from Step 3. (If the fabric has a repeat, multiply the repeat distance by the number of widths and add this figure to the total. The extra fabric will allow you to match the designs.) Divide this number by 36 and round number up to the next ¼ yard to get the total yardage.

Cutting Instructions—Draperies

1. Use a carpenter's square to straighten one end of the decorator and the lining fabrics.

2. Cut the decorator fabric and lining fabric to the cut length determined in Step 4 in Fabric Calculations; make sure designs in fabric lengths match exactly.

Construction—Draperies

Note: Use ½" seam allowance unless otherwise directed.

1. If you determined in Step 3 in Fabric Calculations that more than one width is needed to achieve the cut width, sew the decorator fabric widths together and the lining fabric widths together now. Trim if necessary. Remember to avoid a center seam when stitching widths together. See Stitching Fabric Widths Together, page 97.

2. Trim lining 6" along one selvage and 3" along the bottom.

3. Hem the decorator and lining widths separately. At the bottom of each decorator panel, create a double 4" hem. Fold over and press 8" of fabric toward the wrong side. Next, tuck in the top of the hem 4" to meet the fold. Stitch or fuse hem. To hem the lining fabric, create a double 3" hem. Fold over and press 6" of fabric toward the wrong side. Next, tuck in the top of the hem 3" to meet the fold. Stitch or fuse hem.

4. Place decorator fabric and lining right sides together. Pin together along one side seam. Make sure the top edges of the decorator fabric and lining fabric are even, and that the bottom edge of the lining is 1" shorter than the decorator fabric. Stitch one side seam together (Fig. 2). Press the seam toward the lining.

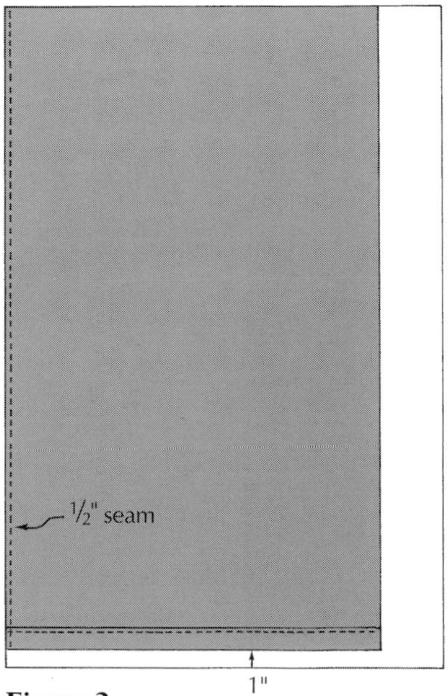

5. Gently pull the lining over to meet the other side of the decorator fabric. Pin this side seam together, and stitch.

6. Turn curtains right sides out. Arrange the curtain so the decorator fabric "wraps" around to the back equally on

½" seam

1"

Figure 2

Materials Needed

From the Fabric Store
- Decorator fabric for draperies (Select a medium-weight 54"-wide decorator fabric, such as broadcloth, chintz, damask, denim, linen, or sateen.)
- Lining fabric, 54" wide
- Decorator fabric for swag scarf
- Thread to match decorator fabrics
- Sew-in "perfect pleater" tape (2½ times rod length)
- Pleater hooks and clips

- Hook rings
- Decorative rod, finials, and brackets (also available in department and hardware stores)
- Dressmaker scissors
- Fabric marking pen or pencil
- Point turner
- Paper-backed fusible tape, for scarf
- *Optional:* Decorative holdbacks

From the Hardware Store
- Carpenter's square

each side from the top of the curtain to the bottom hem (Fig. 3). Press fabric smooth.

7. For a custom hem finish, create mitered corners at the bottom of the decorator panels. With wrong side facing you, diagonally fold *under*—at a 45° angle—the bottom corner of

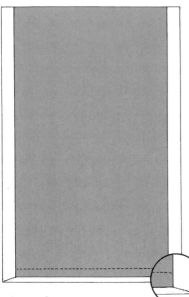

the side hem until the point of each corner meets the side edge *inside the side hem*. Press. Hand stitch in place (Fig. 3).

8. Cut one length of pleater tape slightly longer than the width of each drapery panel; begin and end each length with a non-scored section of tape. Center tape so that first and last scored sections are an equal distance from each side edge. Trim excess tape if necessary so tape is even with drapery panel.

Figure 3

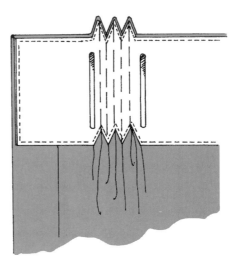

Figure 6

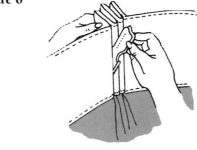

Figure 7

9. On right side of each fabric panel, mark ½" down from upper edge; use fabric marker. Pin tape along marked line so it overlaps the fabric by ½" as shown. Stitch tape to fabric ¼" from edge of tape (Fig. 4).

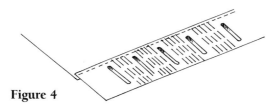

Figure 4

10. Fold tape to inside of curtain and press along top edge. Stitch along lower edge and both sides of tape (Fig. 5).

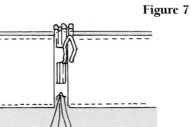

Figure 8

go between tape and fabric (Fig. 7). Then slide clip up firmly into heading to lock in place (Fig. 8). Insert hook into top position on clips.

Installing and "Dressing" the Curtains

1. Place pleated panels on rod; insert hooks into lower rings. You may have to move a ring or two to the outside of the brackets.

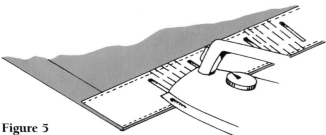

Figure 5

11. To form pleats, fold fabric along pleat lines of tape (Fig. 6). Hold pinched pleat in one hand. Grasp clip with the other hand and insert bottom of clip into slotted openings on tape; push clip down as far as it will

2. To "dress" the panels, push the panels to both sides of the window. Starting from the top, crease the area between the pleats back toward the window. Continue to arrange fabric into evenly spaced soft folds the length of the panels. With 4" wide fabric strips, loosely wrap the panels midway between the header and hem and again just above the hem (Fig. 9). Steam the folds gently with a steam iron or hand-held steamer. Leave the panels tied for a few days to "train" the pleats.

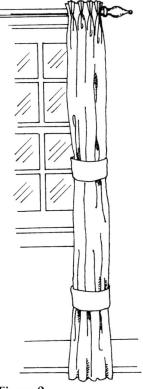

Figure 9

Swag Scarf

Fabric Calculations—Scarf

Note: Any width of fabric can be used for the swag scarf.

1. Measure from the top of the rod to where you'd like the swag scarf to end along the sides. A good length is about ⅓ the length of the under drapes. Multiply this number by 2.

2. Next, measure the length of the rod between brackets. Add together this measurement *plus a third of this measurement.*

3. Add the totals from Step 1 and Step 2 to get the finished length.

4. To determine the cut length, add 7" (for finishing allowance) to the total finished length from Step 3.

5. Divide the cut length by 36 to determine yardage.

Construction—Scarf

1. Trim off fabric selvages.

2. To form the angled ends, mark 3" from upper edges and 15" from lower edges and connect these marks. Carefully cut along these diagonal lines (Fig. 10). Save these triangles; they will be used to line the scarf ends.

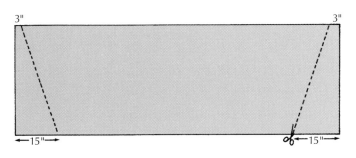

Figure 10

Figure 11

3. Press under ½" toward wrong side along each triangle's long, straight edge (Fig. 11).

4. Place each triangle right sides together with one scarf end; match diagonal edges. Using a 4" seam allowance along straight grain edges and ½" seam allowance along diagonal edge, stitch around the scarf/triangle common outer edges (Fig. 12).

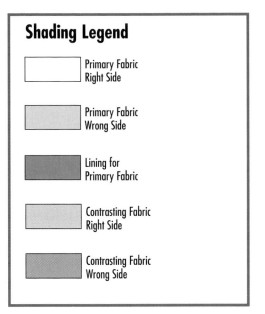

Shading Legend

Primary Fabric Right Side

Primary Fabric Wrong Side

Lining for Primary Fabric

Contrasting Fabric Right Side

Contrasting Fabric Wrong Side

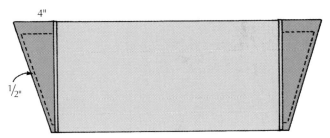

Figure 12

5. Trim the corner seam allowances diagonally. Turn the triangles right side out. Use a point turner and gently push fabric from the inside out to create sharp corners. Press smooth.

6. Press under each long edge of scarf 4" toward wrong side of fabric. Then tuck 2" under to meet fold to create a double 2" hem (Fig. 13). Using a paper-backed fusible tape, fuse hem to scarf. Also place tape between each triangle hemmed edge and the scarf and fuse the two layers together.

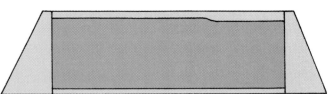

Figure 13

7. From each long point of the scarf, measure and pin the side length measurement. "Scrunch" the fabric together at these points and drape scarf over rod as shown in the photo. Pull the bottom edge of the scarf until you have a pleasing drape (Fig. 14).

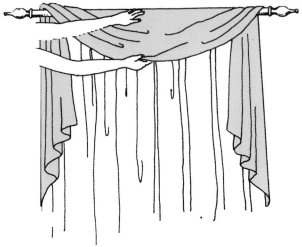

Figure 14

Alternative Design

This treatment is perfect for a large window. Just adjust your measurements accordingly.

Pinafore Curtain

I like this treatment so much that I have it hanging in my living room. The covered buttons along the sides are purely decorative, but my friend Maureen Klein suggested making them functional. By making buttonholes in the pinafore layer and adding buttons to the back layer, you can change the "pinafore." Imagine, changing the look of the treatment on a whim!

This window treatment has a lined "back" panel—the yellow fabric in the photo—and a decorative, unlined "front" panel—the blue plaid fabric in the photo. Contrasting covered buttons are attached down the sides of the curtain.

Techniques to Know Before You Begin

Materials Needed

From the Fabric Store
- Decorator fabric for curtain (Select a medium-weight 54"-wide decorator fabric, such as damask, sateen, linen, or broadcloth.)
- Coordinating decorator fabric for front panel (See guidelines for decorator fabric)
- Contrasting fabric to cover buttons
- Lining fabric

- Thread to match decorator fabrics
- 36 covered button forms, 1⅛" diameter
- Decorative rod, finials and brackets (also available at department and hardware stores)
- Fabric marking pen or pencil
- Dressmaker scissors

From the Hardware Store
- Carpenter's square

Fabric Calculations

Note: These instructions will result in panels that are each 48" wide. This size is suitable for windows up to 60" wide at 1½ times fullness. If your window is wider than 60", you must add the appropriate number of fabric panels to achieve the width and re-calculate the yardage. For help, see Yardage Calculations, p. 94.

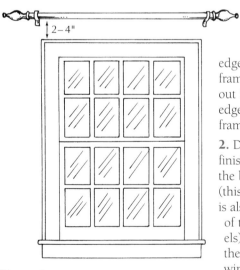

Figure 1

1. Mount the hardware 2 to 4" above the top edge of the window frame and 2 to 4" out from each side edge of the window frame (Fig. 1).

2. Determine the finished length of the back panels (this measurement is also the *cut length* of the front panels). Measure from the top edge of the window frame to the floor. (Note: This window treatment looks great with the bottom of the curtain puddled slightly on the floor. If you want to create this look, add 8 to 12" to the finished length measurement when calculating yardages.)

3. To determine the cut length of the back panels, add 8½" to the finished length for finishing allowance.

4. Determine the total yardage of back panel fabric and lining fabric for back panel. Multiply the cut length by 2 for the second curtain panel. (If the fabric has a repeat, multiply the repeat distance by 2 and add this figure to the total.) Divide this number by 36 and round number up to next ¼ yard.

5. The yardage necessary for the front panels is the total yardage found in Step 4, plus 1 yard for the ties.

Cutting Instructions

1. Use a carpenter's square to straighten one end of all fabrics.

2. Cut the back panel fabric and lining fabric to the cut length determined in Step 3 in Fabric Calculations. Trim each *lining* panel 6" along one selvage and 3" along the bottom.

3. Cut the front panel fabric to the cut length determined in Step 2 in Fabric Calculations.

4. From the front panel fabric, cut 32 lengthwise strips, each 3 by 18" for the ties.

Construction

Note: Use ½" seam allowance unless otherwise directed.
BACK CURTAIN PANEL

1. Hem the decorator and lining panels separately. At the bottom of each decorator panel, create a double 4" hem. Fold over and press 8" of fabric toward the wrong side. Next, tuck in the top of the hem 4" to meet the fold. Stitch or fuse hem. To hem the lining fabric, create a double 3" hem. Fold over and press 6" of fabric toward the wrong side. Next, tuck in the top of the hem 3" to meet the fold. Stitch or fuse hem.

2. Place decorator fabric and lining right sides together. Pin together along one side seam. Make sure the top edges of the decorator fabric and lining fabric are even, and that the bottom edge of the lining is 1" shorter than the decorator fabric. Stitch one side seam together. Press the seam toward the lining (Fig. 2).

3. Gently pull the lining over to meet the other side of the decorator fabric. Pin this side seam together, and again, make sure the top edge of both fabrics are even and the bottom edge of the lining is 1" shorter than the decorator fabric (Fig. 3). Stitch this side seam. Press the seam toward the lining.

4. With the decorator fabric and lining fabric still right sides

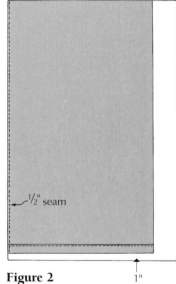

Figure 2

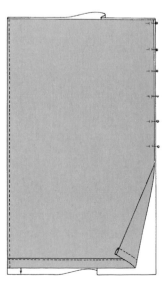

Figure 3

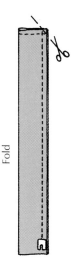

Figure 4

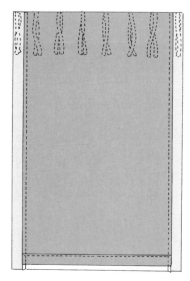

Figure 5

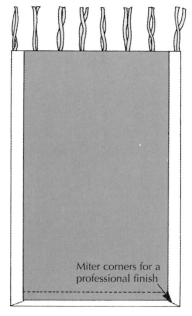

Miter corners for a professional finish

Figure 6

together, place the curtain on a large surface. Arrange the curtain so the decorator fabric "wraps" around to the lining side equally on each side, about 1½". Pin across the top edge to hold in place.

5. To construct ties, fold strips in half lengthwise with right sides together so they measure 1½ by 18". Begin at folded edge and stitch across one short end and the long edge. Clip corners diagonally and trim seam allowances to eliminate bulk (Fig. 4). Turn ties right side out and press flat.

6. Determine the placement of each tab along the top edge of each panel. The first and last tab should be as close to each side as possible; the remaining tabs evenly spaced between these two. Insert the tabs between the lining and the decorator panels with the finished ends of the tab toward the bottom hem (Fig. 5). Be sure the raw edges of the tabs, decorator fabric, and lining fabric are even along the top edge.

7. Stitch through all layers across the top edge. For added reinforcement, stitch again over first stitch line. Clip corners diagonally to eliminate bulk.

8. Turn curtains right sides out. Arrange the curtain so the decorator fabric "wraps" around to the back equally on each side, about 1½". Check that it wraps evenly from the top of the curtain to the bottom hem. Press fabric smooth. (Measure the finished width of the panel and note it. This is the cut width of the front panels.)

9. For a custom hem finish, create mitered corners at the bottom of the decorator panels. With wrong side facing you, diagonally fold *under*—at a 45° angle—the bottom corner of the side hem. The point of each corner meets the side edge *inside the side hem*. Press. Hand stitch in place. (Fig. 6)

FRONT PANEL

1. Trim the front panels so that the width is equal to the finished width of the back panel you measured in Step 8 under Construction—Back Curtain Panel.

2. Hem the front panels; first the top and bottom, and then the sides. Create a double 1½" hem around all of the edges. Fold over and press 3" toward the wrong side. Then tuck under 1½" to meet the fold (Fig. 7). For a professional finish, blind stitch the hem.

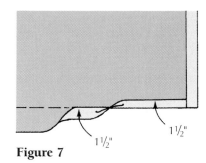

1½"   1½"

Figure 7

FINISHING CURTAINS

1. Lay the back panel right side up on large work surface. Center top panel, also right side up, directly on back panel—the back panel will extend 2" out from all sides of the top panel. Pin to secure around all edges (Fig. 8).

2. Form a tuck along the top edge of the curtain at each tie (except the ones at the edges). To make each tuck, fold the panel right sides together at each tie—include front panel in this fold. Measure in from folded edge 1". Stitch a 5" long seam down from the top edge; backstitch at beginning and end of stitching (Fig. 9).

3. Cover 36 buttons in selected fabric; follow manufacturer's instructions. Each panel requires 18 buttons; 9 on each side.

4. To mark button placement, position each button ½" in from the finished edge of the front panel. Divide the length of the front panel into eight even sections. An easy way to do this is to find the middle point and then divide the sections on either side

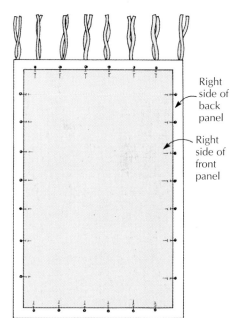

Right side of back panel

Right side of front panel

Figure 8

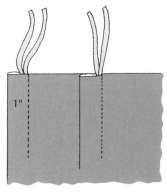

1"

Figure 9

into four smaller sections. Mark button placement.

5. Beginning at the top corner, hand stitch a covered button at each mark through all layers (Fig. 10).

Installing and "Dressing" the Curtain

1. Make a knot or bow with ties. Insert rod through ties and place rod in brackets.

2. Arrange the fabric into folds as desired.

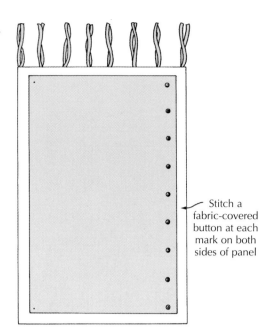

Stitch a fabric-covered button at each mark on both sides of panel

Figure 10

Attached Jabot Valance

*These jabots
add a luscious layer
to basic rod pocket curtains.
This spectacular window
treatment is so easy to make.
I even include instructions
to make cutting the
jabots easier!*

Techniques to Know Before You Begin

The lined jabots in this treatment are constructed separately and then attached to the lined curtains at the rod pocket. The rod is threaded through a simple buttonhole near each end of the header. This allows you to take advantage of a decorative rod and bracket, but still have the return area covered.

Materials Needed

From the Fabric Store
- Decorator fabric for curtain (Select a medium-weight 54"-wide decorator fabric, such as chintz, damask, sateen, linen, or broadcloth.)
- Coordinating decorator fabric for jabot valance (See guidelines for decorator fabric.)
- Lining fabric

- Thread to match both jabot and curtain fabrics
- Decorative rod (1⅜" diameter), finials, and brackets
- Double-stick carpet tape
- Fabric marking pen or pencil
- Dressmaker scissors
- Point turner

From the Hardware Store
- Carpenter's square

Fabric Calculations—Curtains

1. Mount rod 2 to 4" above the top edge of the window frame and 1 to 4" out from each outside edge of the window frame (Fig. 1).

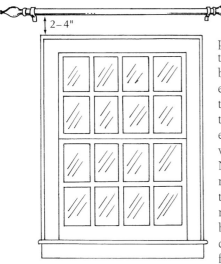

2. To determine the cut width of your panels, first measure the length of the rod between the brackets. Next, measure the return—the distance that the bracket extends from the wall—on each side. Now, add the three measurements together, and then multiply this number by 2½ or 3, depending on the fullness desired.

Figure 1 Finally, add 4" for the side hems and finishing allowance for your total.

3. To determine the number of fabric widths, divide your cut width by the width of fabric you are using. Round to the next whole number.

4. Determine your cut length. Measure from the top of the rod to where you want the curtains to end. (The two best finished lengths are floor-length or to the bottom of the apron.) Add 12" to the measurement for finishing allowance.

5. Determine the total yardage of curtain fabric and lining fabric. Multiply the cut length by the number of widths you need from Step 3. (If you need more than one fabric width and the fabric you have selected has a repeat, multiply the repeat distance by the number of widths and add this figure to the total. The

extra fabric will allow you to match the designs.) Divide this number by 36 and round up to the next ¼ yard.

Fabric Calculations—Jabots

1. Determine the "short point" and the "long point" of the jabot valance. A good short point measurement is 13" and a good long point is 24", but they can be any combination that looks best on your window.

2. To determine the cut length of your jabot, add 1" for seam allowances to the long point measurement.

3. You need the same number of fabric widths for the jabot as for the curtain, determined in Step 3 Fabric Calculations—Curtains.

4. Determine the total yardage of fabric for the jabots and their lining. Multiply the number of widths you need by the cut length from Step 2. (If you need more than one fabric panel and the fabric you have selected has a repeat, multiply the repeat distance by the number of widths and add this figure to the total. The extra fabric will allow you to match the designs.) Divide this number by 36 and round up to the next ¼ yard.

Cutting Instructions—Curtains

1. Use a carpenter's square to straighten one end of the decorator fabric and the lining fabric.

2. Cut fabric panels to the cut length determined in Step 4 in Fabric Calculations—Curtains. Make sure designs in panels match exactly.

Cutting Instructions—Jabots

Note: Cut the jabots after the curtains are completely finished. This will ensure an exact fit.

1. Use a carpenter's square to straighten one end of the decorator fabric.

2. Cut fabric widths to the cut length determined in Step 2 in Fabric Calculations—Jabots; make sure the designs in the widths match exactly.

3. If you determined in Step 3 in Fabric Calculations—Jabots that you need more than one fabric width to achieve the cut width, sew the decorator fabric widths together and the lining fabric widths together now. Remember to avoid a center seam when sewing fabric widths together. See Stitching Fabric Widths Together, page 97.

4. Determine the correct cut width of the jabot. Measure the finished width of the stitched-and-hemmed curtain panel to be sure its size hasn't changed during the sewing process. Add 1" for seam allowances. Now trim each jabot to the precise cut width.

5. Along one side edge, measure down the short point measurement plus 1". Mark. Along opposite edge, measure down the long point measurement plus 1" (Fig. 2). Mark. Connect the two points together with a diagonal line. Cut along all marked lines.

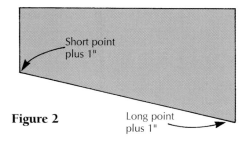

Figure 2

Short point plus 1"

Long point plus 1"

6. Cut out second jabot using the same measurements; make sure the right sides of the short points of the jabots are facing each other (Fig. 3). (Avoid making two "left" or two "right" jabots.)

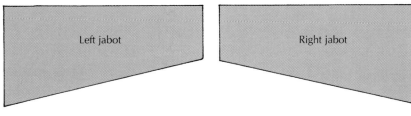

Left jabot

Right jabot

Figure 3

7. Cut two lining layers the exact same size and shape as the decorator fabrics.

Construction—Curtains

Note: Use ¹/₂" seam allowance unless otherwise directed.

1. If you determined in Step 3 in Fabric Calculations—Curtains that more than one width is needed to achieve the cut width for your curtain panel, sew the decorator fabric widths together and the lining fabric widths together now. Trim if necessary. Remember to avoid a center seam when sewing fabric widths together. See Stitching Fabric Widths Together, page 97.

2. Trim lining 6" along one selvage and 3" along bottom edge.

3. Hem the decorator and lining panels separately. At the bottom of each decorator panel, create a double 4" hem. Fold over and press 8" of fabric toward the wrong side. Next, tuck in the top of the hem 4" to meet the

Cutting Jabots Quickly and Easily

✂You can cut out a pair of jabots quickly and easily by layering the decorator fabric and the lining *right sides together*. You need two pieces of decorator fabric and two pieces of lining fabric. The first and second layers are the first jabot; the second and third are the second jabot. Follow these steps *exactly* or you'll end up with two right or two left jabots!

• Lay first piece of decorator fabric right side up on a large work surface.
• Lay first piece of lining fabric right side down on top of decorator fabric.
• Lay second piece of lining right side up on top of first piece of lining fabric.
• Lay decorator fabric right side down on top of second piece of lining.

Make sure that all selvages are even. Pin layers together. Now measure and cut out jabots as instructed!

fold. Stitch or fuse hem. To hem the lining fabric, create a double 3" hem. Fold over and press 6" of fabric toward the wrong side. Next, tuck in the top of the hem 3" to meet the fold. Stitch or fuse hem.

4. Place decorator fabric and lining right sides together. Pin together along one side seam. Make sure the top edges of

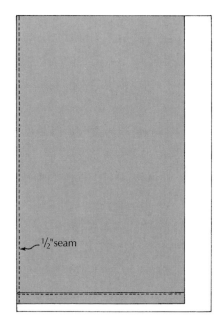

¹/₂" seam

Figure 4

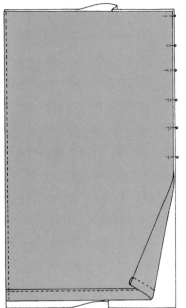

Figure 5

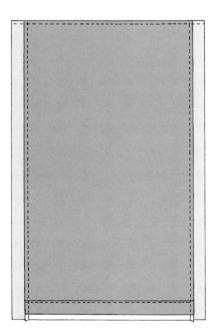

Figure 6

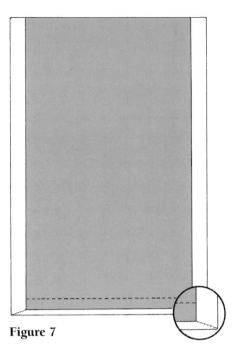

Figure 7

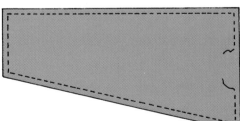

Figure 8

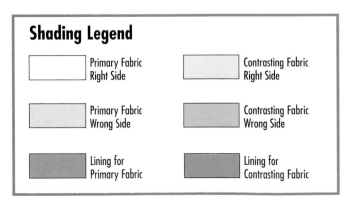

the decorator fabric and lining fabric are even, and that the bottom edge of the lining is 1" shorter than the decorator fabric. Stitch one side seam together (Fig. 4). Press the seam toward the lining.

5. Gently pull the lining over to meet the other side of the decorator fabric. Pin this side seam together, and stitch. Press the seam toward the lining (Fig. 5).

6. With the decorator fabric and lining fabric still right sides together, place the curtain on a large surface. Arrange the curtain so the decorator fabric "wraps" around to the lining side equally on each side, about 1½". Pin across the top edge to hold in place. Stitch across the top edge (Fig. 6).

7. Clip corners diagonally to eliminate bulk. Turn curtains right sides out. Arrange the curtain so the decorator fabric "wraps" around to the back equally on each side from the top of the curtain to the bottom hem. Press fabric smooth.

8. For a custom hem finish, create mitered corners at the bottom of the decorator panels. With wrong side facing you, diagonally fold under—at a 45° angle—the bottom corner of the side hem until the point of each corner meets the side edge *inside the side hem*. Press. Hand stitch in place (Fig. 7).

Construction—Jabots

1. Place jabots and lining right sides together. Stitch around all sides; leave an 8" opening on the long side edge for turning (Fig. 8). Clip corners diagonally to eliminate bulk.

Leave open for turning

2. Use a point turner to push the fabric out and create sharp points. Turn jabots right sides out and press smooth.

3. Fuse or hand stitch the opening closed.

Finishing Curtains

1. Lay jabots right side up on a large work surface. On the return side of each jabot (the longer side), mark the position of the buttonhole. Measure ¼" down from top edge and measure in the return distance that was determined in Step 2 in Fabric Calculations—Curtains. Mark. This is the top of the buttonhole. Stitch a vertical 2¾" long buttonhole at this mark (Fig. 9). Carefully cut open the buttonhole.

Shading Legend

- Primary Fabric Right Side
- Primary Fabric Wrong Side
- Lining for Primary Fabric
- Contrasting Fabric Right Side
- Contrasting Fabric Wrong Side
- Lining for Contrasting Fabric

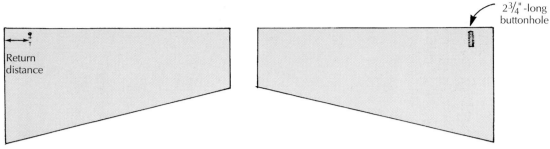

Figure 9

2. Lay curtain right side up on large work surface. Lay jabot directly on top of curtain, also right side up. The top edge of the curtain should extend 2½" above the top edge of the jabot. Pin to secure around all edges (Fig. 10).

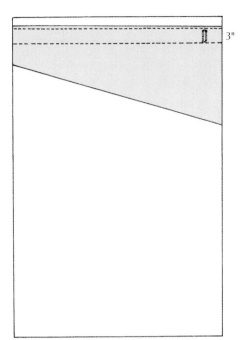

Figure 11

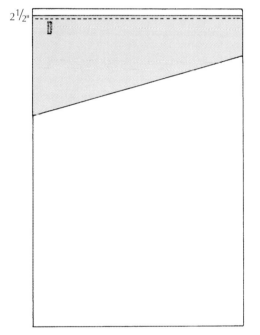

Figure 10

3. Carefully stitch along the top edge of the jabot; stitch as close to the finished edge as possible.

4. Measure down 3" from the first stitch line; mark with fabric marker. Stitch along this line to form the bottom of the rod pocket (Fig. 11).

Installing and "Dressing" the Curtain

1. Slide rod through rod pocket. The end of each rod should exit through the buttonhole at each side.

2. Place rod in brackets and arrange the return around the sides neatly. Place the double-stick carpet tape to the inside area of the bracket so that it meets the edge of the curtain along the return as shown in Fig. 12.

3. Return rod to brackets and secure in place. Arrange the fabric into folds as desired.

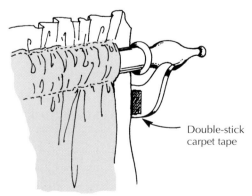

Double-stick carpet tape

Figure 12

Cuffed Curtain

You'll have fun selecting two coordinating fabrics for this easy-to-make style. I created this treatment in a one-panel asymmetrical style with optional puddling, but it works just as well as a two-paneled treatment draped along both sides of a window.

The cuff for this treatment is created separately and can be made from a coordinating fabric. The entire treatment is suspended from rings on a decorative rod.

Fabric Calculations— Curtain and Lining

1. Install hardware 2 to 4" above the top edge of the window frame and 1 to 4" out from each outside edge of the window frame (Fig. 1). Place rings on rod.

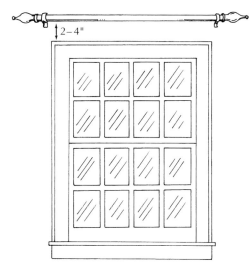

Figure 1

2. To determine the cut width of the fabric, measure the rod from bracket to bracket. Multiply this number by 2½ for adequate fullness. Now add 4" to your total for side hems.

3. Determine the number of fabric widths you need to achieve the cut width. Divide the cut width by the width of fabric you are using. Round up to the next whole number.

4. Determine your cut length. Measure from the bottom of the ring to the floor. Add 8½" for the hem and seam allowance. If you want to "puddle" the curtain on the floor, add an extra 12 to 15".

Materials Needed

From the Fabric Store
- Decorator fabric for curtain (Select a medium-weight 54"-wide decorator fabric, such as damask, denim, sateen, linen, or broadcloth.)
- Lining fabric for curtain
- Coordinating decorator fabric for cuff (See guidelines for decorator fabric)
- Lining fabric for cuff
- Thread to match decorator fabrics

- Decorative wooden pole set (1³/8" diameter) and brackets
- Wooden or plastic rings, 2" diameter
- Fabric marking pen or pencil
- Dressmaker scissors

From the Hardware Store
- Carpenter's square

5. Determine the total yardage of the curtain and lining fabrics. First, multiply the number of widths you need by the cut length from Step 4. (If you need more than one fabric width and the fabric you have selected has a repeat, multiply the repeat distance by the number of widths and add this figure to the total. The extra fabric will allow you to match the designs.) Second, multiply the number of widths you need by 5" (for the facing). Third, add these two numbers together. Now, divide your total by 36, and round up to the next ¼ yard.

Fabric Calculations— Contrasting Cuff and Cuff Lining

1. The cut width of the cuff is the same as the cut width of the curtain as found in Step 2 in Fabric Calculations—Curtain and Lining.

2. You need the same number of widths for the cuff as you do for the curtain, found in Step 3 in Fabric Calculations—Curtain and Lining.

3. Decide the cut length of the cuff; it can vary from 7 to 13". The cuff in the photo has a cut length of 13".

4. To determine the yardage for the cuff and its lining, multiply the number of widths needed by the cut length. (If you need more than one fabric width and the fabric you have selected has a repeat, multiply the repeat distance by the number of widths and add this figure to the total. The extra fabric will allow you to match the designs.). Divide by 36 and round up to the next ¼ yard.

Construction—Curtain

Note: Directions are given for making a one-panel asymmetrical window treatment. Use ½" seam allowance unless otherwise noted.

1. Straighten one end of the fabrics by using a carpenter's square.

2. Cut the fabric and the lining to the cut length determined in Step 4, Fabric Calculations—Curtain and Lining; make sure designs in fabric lengths match exactly. If you determined you need more than one fabric width to achieve the cut width, sew the decorator fabric widths together and the lining fabric widths together now. Trim if necessary. Remember to avoid a center seam when stitching fabric widths together. For help, see Stitching Fabric Widths Together, page 97.

3. Trim *lining* 6" along one selvage and 3" along the bottom.

4. Hem the decorator and lining fabrics separately. At the bottom of the decorator panel, create a double 4" hem. Fold over and press

8" of fabric toward the wrong side. Next, tuck in the top of the hem 4" to meet the fold. Stitch or fuse hem. To hem the lining, create a double 3" hem. Fold over and press 6" of fabric toward the wrong side. Next, tuck in the top of the hem 3" to meet the fold.

5. Place decorator fabric and lining right sides together. Pin together along one side seam. Make sure the top edges of both layers are even, and that the bottom edge of the lining is 1" shorter than the decorator fabric. Stitch one side seam together (Fig. 2). Press

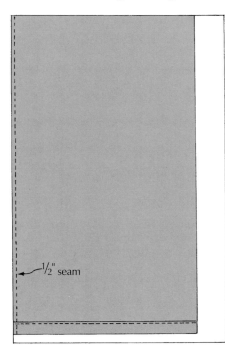

Figure 2

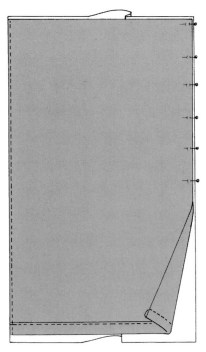

Figure 3

the seam toward the lining.

6. Gently pull the lining over to meet the other side of the decorator fabric. Pin this side seam together, and stitch (Fig. 3). Press the seam toward the lining.

7. Turn curtains right side out. Arrange the curtain so the decorator fabric "wraps" around to the back equally on each side. Check that it wraps evenly from the top of the curtain to the bottom hem. Press fabric smooth. *Measure the finished width of the curtain panel and note it.*

8. For a custom hem finish, create mitered corners at the bottom of the decorator panels. With wrong side facing you, diagonally fold *under*—at a 45° angle—the bottom corner of the side hem until the point of each corner meets the side edge *inside the side hem*. Press. Hand stitch in place (Fig. 4).

9. Set curtain aside as you prepare the cuff.

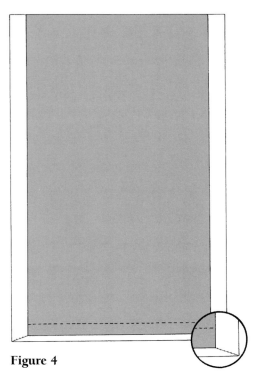

Figure 4

Construction—Cuff

1. Cut the cuff fabric and the cuff lining fabric to the cut length determined in Step 3, in Fabric Calculations—Contrasting Cuff and Cuff Lining. If you determined you need more than one fabric width to achieve the cut width, sew the decorator fabric widths together and the lining fabric widths together now. Remember to avoid a center seam when stitching fabric widths together. For help, see Stitching Fabric Widths Together, page 97.

2. Trim cuff and lining fabrics so that their cut width is equal to the finished width of the curtain (Step 8 in Construction—Curtain) *plus 1"*.

3. Pin cuff and lining fabrics right sides together. In a continuous stitching line, stitch down one short end, across the entire width of the cuff, and up the opposite short end.

4. Clip the completely stitched corners diagonally to remove bulk (Fig. 5). Turn unit right sides out and press smooth.

TIP: Add a contrasting fabric band to the edges of the curtain and the cuff. Fringe, piping, or trim are all suitable.

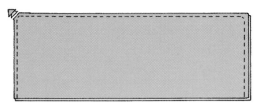

Figure 5

Attaching Cuff to Curtain

1. Prepare the facing strips. Trim each strip so that it is equal to the finished width of the panel in Step 9 in Construction—Curtain plus 1". Press under ½" on each side. Also press under ½" on one long side.

2. Place the lining side of the cuff to the right side of the curtain. The cuff should be the exact same width as the curtain (Fig. 6).

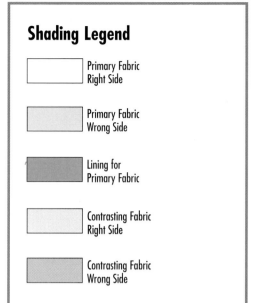

Shading Legend

Primary Fabric
Right Side

Primary Fabric
Wrong Side

Lining for
Primary Fabric

Contrasting Fabric
Right Side

Contrasting Fabric
Wrong Side

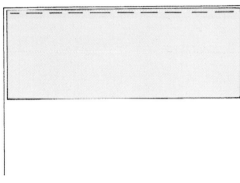

Figure 6

3. Pin facing to upper edge of cuff, right sides together (the cuff is sandwiched between the facing and the curtain). All edges should be even. Stitch through all layers along upper edge (Fig. 7). Grade seams.

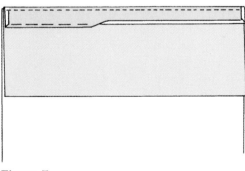

Figure 7

4. Open curtain flat so cuff extends away from curtain. Press facing to wrong side of curtain. Stitch facing to curtain along long edge and sides (Fig. 8).

5. Determine the placement of each ring along the top edge of the curtain. The first

Figure 8

and last rings should be at top corners; space additional rings approximately 6 to 8" apart.

6. Hand stitch a ring securely at each of these points (Fig. 9).

Installing and "Dressing" the Curtain

1. Slide rings onto rod and place rod in brackets. To duplicate the look shown, gently gather the curtain over to one side and hold in place with cording or any style of tieback.

2. Arrange the folds evenly across the top.

3. To keep the curtain from sliding all the way over to the side, insert a small tack nail

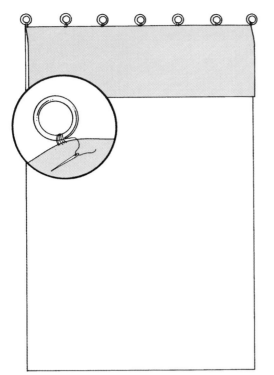

Figure 9

into the rod beside each ring. Be sure the nail is on the side of the ring to which the curtain will be drawn. The nails will act as "brakes" and will keep the curtain in place.

Alternative Design

You can make this curtain as two individual panels. One 54" width of fabric per panel is sufficient for windows up to 60" wide at 1½ times fullness. If you want a fuller curtain, simply stitch fabric widths together to achieve your desired fullness.

Knotted Scarf

This window treatment will add a look of sophistication to any room. The covered rod is an elegant touch; the wide fabric band is a functional embellishment. Indulge yourself with this nontraditional window treatment.

Techniques to Know Before You Begin

Each panel of this treatment is a single, lined width of fabric that is draped over the rod and wrapped with a fabric band. The coordinating lining (the dark green fabric in the photo) forms the back of each panel, which can be designed to show as little or as much as you prefer. The treatment is suspended from a plain rod which is covered with a rounded curtain-rod cover and then a fabric "sleeve."

Materials Needed

From the Fabric Store
- Decorator fabric for curtain (Select a medium-weight 54"-wide decorator fabric, such as damask, denim, sateen, linen, or broadcloth.)
- Coordinating decorator fabric for lining (See guidelines for decorator fabric.)
- Thread to match decorator fabric
- Rounded curtain-rod cover, such as Pinnacle or Continental Plus
- 2¹/₂"-wide flat rod with returns
- Stitch-in hook-and-loop tape
- Dressmaker scissors

From the Hardware Store
- Carpenter's square

Fabric Calculations

1. Install hardware 2 to 4" above the top edge of the window frame and 2 to 4" out from each outside edge of window frame (Fig. 1).

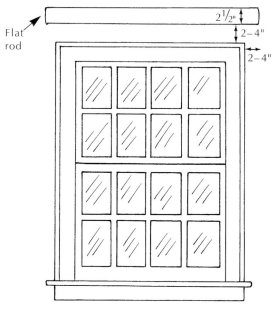

Figure 1

2. To determine the cut length of each scarf, first measure from the floor up, over the rod, and down to where you would like the front part of the scarf to end. Then add 3" to this measurement.

3. Determine the yardage of the decorator fabric. If the fabric has a repeat, add this measurement to the cut length.

4. Multiply the total in Step 3 by 2 for rod lengths up to 48". Then add increments of 18" for longer rods.

5. To the total of Step 4, add 36" for the rod covering.

6. To the total of Step 5, add 21" for the bands.

7. Divide the total of Step 6 by 36 and round up to the next ¹/₄ yard. This is the total yardage.

8. Repeat Steps 2, 3, and 4 to determine the yardage for the coordinating lining fabric.

Cutting Instructions

1. Use a carpenter's square to straighten one end of the decorator fabric and the coordinating lining fabric.

2. Cut the decorator fabric and the coordinating lining fabric to the cut length determined in Step 2 in Fabric Calculations; make sure designs in fabric lengths match exactly.

3. Trim selvages from decorator fabric and lining fabric. Use the entire width of the fabric for each panel.

4. Form the diagonal ends of the scarf. Place decorator panel and lining panel right sides together. At the top edge, measure in 12" from each side. Mark. Draw a line from this mark to the bottom corner (Fig. 2). Cut along these lines and discard the triangles. Put panels aside.

Figure 2

5. Cut out the rod sleeve. From the decorator fabric, cut at least two strips, each 18 by 54".

6. Cut out the bands. From the decorator fabric cut two strips, each 11 by 21".

7. Cut hook-and-loop tape into two strips, each 5" long.

Construction

Note: Use ¹/₂" seam allowance unless otherwise noted.

SCARF

1. Stitch lining and decorator fabrics together along all sides. Leave a 10" opening along the upper straight edge for turning.

2. Trim corners diagonally to eliminate bulk. Turn scarf right side out and press smooth

3. Hand stitch or fuse the opening closed.

BANDS

1. Fold each of the 11 by 21" strips in half lengthwise with right sides together.

Beginning at folded edge, stitch along all three sides; leave a 4" opening along the longest edge for turning (Fig. 3).

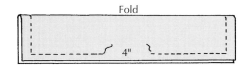

Fold

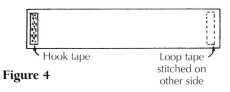

4"

Figure 3

2. Trim corners diagonally to eliminate bulk. Turn bands right side out and press smooth. Hand stitch or fuse the opening closed.

3. Separate hook-and-loop tape. Stitch one part to one end and its mate to the opposite end *and the opposite side* of the band (see Fig. 4).

Hook tape

Loop tape stitched on other side

Figure 4

ROD SLEEVE

1. Form one long strip with the 18 by 54" strips. Place short ends right sides together and stitch. Press seam open.

2. On each short end of this long strip, press under ½" toward wrong side of fabric. Press under another ½" and stitch hem in place (Fig. 5)

Figure 5

3. Fold strip in half lengthwise with right sides together. Stitch along longest side to form one long tube, leaving an opening for turning. Press seam open.

4. Turn sleeve right side out and press sleeve smooth, but not flat.

Installing and "Dressing" the Curtain

1. Remove flat rod from brackets. Slide rounded curtain-rod cover over flat rod. Slide the rod sleeve onto rod; position seam so that it is against the wall. Distribute gathers evenly.

2. Arrange the scarf into folds at the point where the fabric will drape over the rod.

3. Drape the scarf over the rod; make sure both sides are even. Arrange the folds in a pleasing arrangement.

4. "Scrunch" the fabric together under the rod. Wrap band around scarf. Arrange gathers and folds as desired (Fig. 6).

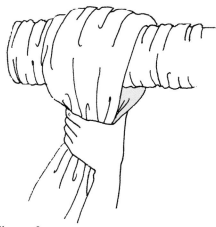

Figure 6

Alternative Design

There are many alternatives to this design. Here are a few of them! Change the length and shape of the ends of the curtain for a completely different look. Cut the ends of the front of the scarf into a graceful V shape and puddle the ends of the back of the scarf on the floor. Or, add piping along the edges for a professional touch.

Scalloped Valance

This is my mom's favorite window treatment—I see another project in my future! However, because it's so simple to put together, making it for her dining room will be a snap. This style is easily adapted to windows of various sizes; just add scallops in the center. Contrasting fabric-covered piping and covered buttons provide the perfect accent for this elegant valance.

Each scallop is made individually, then attached to a mounting board. Patterns for each scallop are drafted from templates provided. Instructions for panel curtains shown in photo are given on page 25.

Techniques to Know Before You Begin

Planning Your Valance

1. Determine the length of the mounting board. If window has a frame, measure the width of the window from outside frame edge to outside frame edge. Add 1" if not using side curtain panels; 2" if using side curtain panels. If the window does not have a frame, measure the opening and add 2" if not using side curtain panels; 3" if using side curtain panels.

2. Prepare mounting board either by painting it to match the wall color or by covering the board with decorator fabric.

3. Install the mounting board 2 to 4" above the window like a shelf; use angle brackets to secure board to wall (Fig. 1). Note: Do not

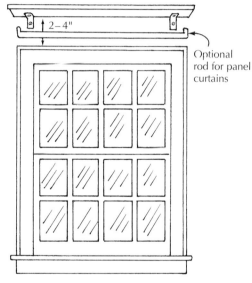

Figure 1

Materials Needed

From the Fabric Store
- Decorator fabric (Select a medium-weight 54"-wide decorator fabric, such as broadcloth, chintz, damask, linen, or sateen.)
- Contrasting fabric to cover buttons and cover cording
- Lining fabric
- Thread to match decorator fabrics
- 10 yards cording (⁵/32)
- 10 covered button forms, ⁷/8"diameter (or one for each scallop)
- Dressmaker scissors

- Large pieces of tracing paper for pattern
- Point turner
- Standard flat curtain rod (if using panel curtains)
- *Optional:* double-fold bias tape

From the Hardware Store
- Mounting board
- Angle brackets (at least 2, and then 1 for each 36")
- Screws, 2" long (2–4 for each angle bracket)
- Push pins
- Heavy-duty staple gun with ¹/2" staples
- Carpenter's square

yet permanently attach the board to the brackets.

4. If you will use panel curtains with this valance, you need to plan for that rod placement at this time. Use a standard flat curtain rod, and mount it slightly below and just outside the angle brackets for the mounting board, as shown. When the valance and the curtains are installed, the sides and top of the panel curtains should be obscured by the valance.

5. Make full-size paper patterns to determine the number of scallops and the arrangement of the shapes, and to make adjustments to the suggested pattern dimensions. On tracing paper and using the diagrams on pages 74 and 75, draft two each of the five suggested shapes. These shapes do not include any seam allowances—they will be added when the shapes are cut out. The returns on the patterns are designed for a 1-by-4" mounting board, but they can be adjusted to fit any size mounting board.

6. Remove the mounting board and find the center of the board. Begin by taping the two "A" shapes at the center (Fig. 2). Then fill in the remaining area by overlapping shapes "B", "C", "D", and"E". Adjust the overlap so the shapes create a valance that is proportional to the window. Make sure the end pieces go around the return and the sides are flush with the wall (Fig. 3).

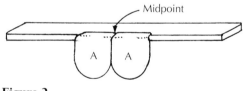

Figure 2

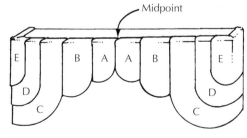

Figure 3

Note: If you are covering an extra-wide window you may need to add more "A" shapes in the center of the board.

7. When you have determined the arrangement, make any notes that will help you during final installation. Remove the patterns and take them to the fabric store to determine the

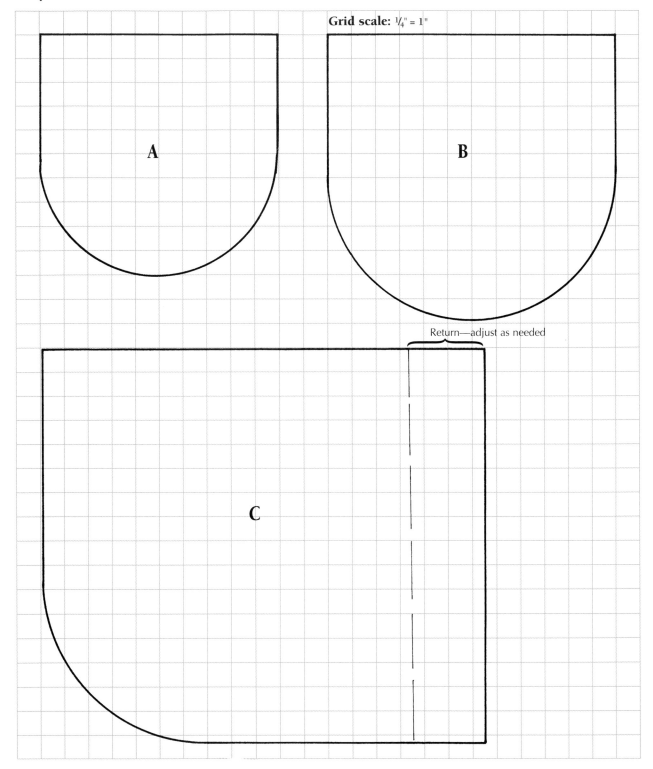

Grid scale: ¼" = 1"

A

B

Return—adjust as needed

C

yardage needed. Match plaids, stripes, and motifs if necessary when planning fabric yardage.

8. Purchase the same amount of lining fabric.

9. Purchase about 10 yards of cording for the ten scallops shown, more if you created more scallops.

10. Purchase fabric to cover the cording. One yard of 54" fabric will yield 20 yards of bias strips to cover the cord.

Note: Depending on the orientation of your window, you may need to interline shapes "A", "B", and"C" to prevent light from showing through, or use blackout lining.

Construction

Note: All seam allowances are ½" unless otherwise noted.

1. Cut bias strips 1¼" wide to cover cording. Make piping (see p. 100).

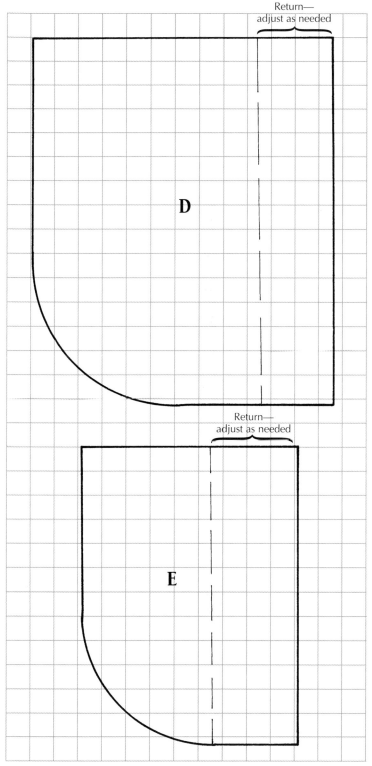

Figure 4

Figure 5

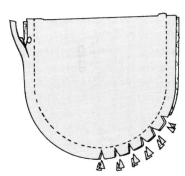

Figure 6

2. Using the paper patterns, cut shapes from the decorator and lining fabrics. *Important:* Add 1/2" seam allowance around entire perimeter when cutting fabric!

3. Lay piping on right side of decorator fabric; match raw edges. Machine baste piping to outside edges of each scallop shape; use zipper foot or special piping foot (Fig. 4).

4. Place decorator and lining fabrics right sides together; piping is between the two layers. Carefully flip the scallops over so you can see the basting stitches that hold the piping to the top. Pin layers together.

5. Stitch around scallop (leave the top edge open), between the basting line that secured piping in place and the actual cord (Fig. 5).

6. Turn scallop right side out to make sure piping is tight in the seam. If it is not, stitch again closer to the edge of the piping. Trim the seam allowance to 1/4" to eliminate bulk. Notch the curved seams (Fig. 6). Turn scallop right side out; use a point turner to gently push the fabric out to create smooth, round curves. Press smooth.

7. On a large work surface, arrange scallops right side up in planned configuration. Pin together. Stitch across the top edge to secure. Clean finish top edge by either serging, overcast stitching, or enclosing the seam in bias tape.

8. Cover buttons with contrasting fabric. Hand tack buttons where desired along top inside edge of each shape (refer to photograph).

Installing the Valance

Note: If mounting valance over panel curtains, mount panel curtains first, then valance.

1. Staple scallops to board; start in center and work toward each side. Miter the corner neatly when forming the return (Fig. 7).

2. Place mounting board with attached scal-

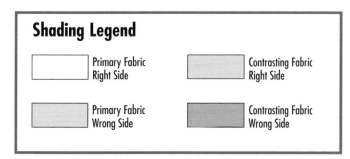

Shading Legend

☐ Primary Fabric Right Side	☐ Contrasting Fabric Right Side
☐ Primary Fabric Wrong Side	☐ Contrasting Fabric Wrong Side

lops over angle brackets and screw angle
bracket to board.

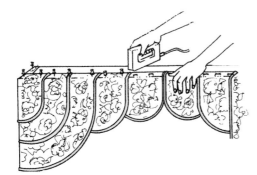

Figure 7

Alternative Design

**Consider using two coordinating fabrics—one for the valance and
one for the panel curtains—to emphasize the design.**

Two-Tone Petal Valance

Elegance at its finest! Two coordinating fabrics are used to create this stunning treatment. The petals are layered onto a mounting board, and embellished with covered buttons.

Techniques to Know Before You Begin

Each petal is made individually, then overlapped together on a mounting board. The front petals are self-lined; the back petals are lined with a separate fabric. Patterns for the petals are drafted from templates provided.

Materials Needed

From the Fabric Store

- Decorator fabric for front petals (Select a medium-weight 54"-wide decorator fabric, such as broadcloth, chintz, damask, linen, or sateen.)
- Contrasting fabric for back petals (See guidelines for front petals.)
- Lining for back panels
- Thread to match decorator fabrics
- Covered button forms, 7/8" diameter (see "Petal Chart" for amount)
- Dressmaker scissors

- Large pieces of tracing paper for pattern
- Fabric marking pen or pencil
- Point turner
- Standard flat curtain rod (if using panel curtains)

From the Hardware Store

- 1 × 4" mounting board
- Angle bracket (at least 2, and then 1 for each 36")
- Screws, 2" long (2–4 for each angle bracket)
- Push pins
- Heavy-duty staple gun with 1/2" staples
- Carpenter's square

Planning Your Valance

1. Determine the length of your mounting board. Measure the width of the window from outside frame edge to outside frame edge. Refer to "Petal Chart" and locate number that is the closest *larger* number to your window measurement.

2. Prepare mounting board either by painting it to match the wall color or by covering the board with decorator fabric.

3. Install mounting board 2 to 4" above the window like a shelf; use angle brackets to secure board to wall. Note: Do not yet permanently attach the board to the brackets (Fig. 1).

4. Make full-size paper patterns to double-check the number of petals and their arrangement, and to make adjustments to the suggested pattern dimensions. On tracing paper and using the diagrams on page 79, draft two end petals and the suggested number of front and back petals for your window width. These shapes do not include any seam allowances—they will be added when the shapes are cut out.

5. Remove the mounting board and use push pins to attach the petal patterns to the board. Make sure the end pieces go around the returns and the sides are flush with the wall. Make any adjustments to the pattern pieces now. Remember, the pattern pieces are the finished size—no seam allowances have been added.

6. When you have completed the arrangement, make any notes that will help you during final installation. Remove the pattern from the board, and separate the individual pieces. Take them to the fabric store to match

Petal Chart

Cut Length Mounting Board	Number of Front Petals	Number of Back Petals	Number of Ends	Number of Covered Buttons
36"	3	4	2	4
45"	4	5	2	5
54"	5	6	2	6
63"	6	7	2	7
72"	7	8	2	8
81"	8	9	2	9

plaids, stripes, and motifs if necessary, and determine yardage.

7. Remember, the front petals are self-lined, so be sure to purchase twice the amount of fabric necessary for the front petals. The back petals are lined with lining fabric, so purchase appropriate fabric yardage for the back petals, and the same amount of lining fabric.

Construction

Note: All seam allowances are 1/2" unless otherwise noted.

1. Use a carpenter's square to straighten one end of all fabrics.

2. Using the paper patterns, cut front petals and self-lining from the decorator fabric. Cut

Figure 1

the back petals and lining from the contrasting fabric and lining fabric. *Important:* Add 1/2" seam allowance around entire perimeter when cutting fabric!

3. Place right sides together. Stitch around petal shape; leave the top edge open.

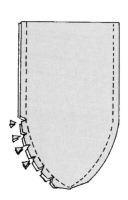

Figure 2

4. Clip corners diagonally and trim seam allowance to 1/4" to eliminate bulk. Notch the curved seams (Fig. 2).

5. Turn shapes right side out; use a point turner to gently push the fabric out to create smooth, round curves. Press smooth.

6. On a large work surface, arrange back petals right side up and side by side with edges touching lightly. Lay front petals on top of back petals so that the back petals are centered behind front petals. On each end, add the end pieces. Baste along top edge (Fig. 3).

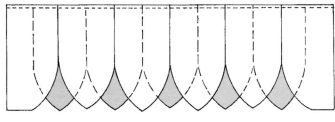

Figure 3

7. Check petal arrangement to see if it fits the board. Make any adjustments now. Stitch along top edge to secure, and clean finish top edge by either serging, overcast stitching, or enclosing the raw edges in bias tape.

8. Cover buttons with contrasting fabric. Hand tack buttons 1" down from top edge and between each top petal (refer to photograph).

Shading Legend

☐	Primary Fabric Right Side	▨	Contrasting Fabric Right Side
▨	Primary Fabric Wrong Side	▨	Contrasting Fabric Wrong Side
▨	Lining for Primary Fabric	▨	Lining For Contrasting Fabric

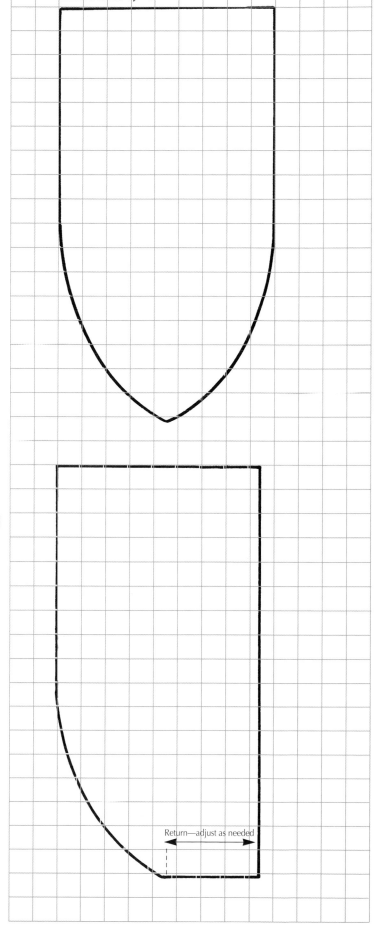

Grid scale: 1/4" = 1"

Return—adjust as needed

Installing the Valance

1. Arrange petal valance on board; the upper edges of each petal should overlap the board by ½". Hold the valance in place with push pins. Make sure the buttons are straight across the board.

2. Staple valance to board; start in center and work toward each side. Miter the corner neatly when forming the return (Fig. 4).

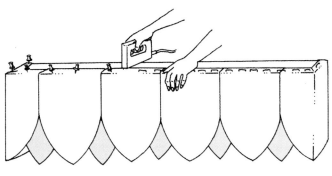

Figure 4

3. Place mounting board over angle brackets and screw angle bracket to board.

Alternative Design

This petal valance looks smashing on a decorative rod. Determine how many 9" wide petals you need to fit the length of your rod (no return pieces are used). Make the petals as instructed, and create a rod pocket. Stitch it to the wrong side of the top edge and insert the rod through the pocket. Consider using a wonderful print and center the main motif in each top petal.

Pointed Valance

This fun window treatment gets its personality from your choice of fabric. I used a striped fabric as the top layer with bits of denim peeking out from between the points. A floral or an ethnic print would give this treatment an entirely different feel.

The finished look of this valance belies its simplicity. After sewing the lined triangles, simply position them and staple them to a mounting board.

Techniques to Know Before You Begin

Materials Needed

From the Fabric Store

- Decorator fabric for the top layer (Select a medium-weight 54"-wide decorator fabric, such as broadcloth, chintz, damask, linen, or sateen.)
- Coordinating fabric for the under layer (See guidelines for decorator fabric.)
- Lining for both the top and bottom layers
- Thread to match decorator fabrics
- Dressmaker scissors
- Large pieces of tracing paper for pattern
- 6"-wide quilt ruler with 30°-angle mark
- Fabric marking pen or pencil
- Point turner
- *Optional:* Bias binding

From the Hardware Store

- 1×4" mounting board
- Push pins
- Carpenter's square
- Angle bracket (at least 2, and then 1 for each 36")
- Screws, 2" long (2–4 for each angle bracket)
- Heavy-duty staple gun with ½" staples

Planning Your Valance

1. Determine the length of your mounting board. If window has a frame, measure the width of the window from outside frame edge to outside frame edge and add 1". If window does not have a frame, measure the opening and add 2".

2. Prepare mounting board by either painting it to match the wall color or by covering the board with decorator fabric.

3. Install mounting board 2 to 4" above the window like a shelf; use angle brackets to secure board to wall (Fig. 1). Note: Do not yet permanently attach the board to the brackets.

4. Make full-size paper triangles to determine the number of triangles and their arrangement. Refer to "Creating Triangles."

5. Arrange top layer triangle patterns into configuration; use length of the board as a guide. Tape together. Now arrange contrasting triangles in place under top layer; tape together. When design appears correct, use push pins to attach your "paper valance" to the mounting board; wrap the outside triangles around returns. Trim end pattern pieces to fit smoothly against the wall.

6. Make any notes that will help you during final installation. Remove the pattern from the board, and separate the individual pieces. Take them to the fabric store and match plaids, stripes, and motifs if necessary, and determine yardage.

7. Purchase the same amount of lining fabric.

Construction

Note: All seam allowances are ¹/₂" unless otherwise noted.

1. Pin paper patterns to the right side of decorator fabrics. Cut around each shape (Fig. 4a). *Important:* Add ¹/₂" seam

Figure 1

Creating Triangles

❧ These instructions produce a 90° triangle with a finished length of 17". The paper pattern does not include seam allowances; they will be added when the shapes are cut out of the fabric.

To make a 90° triangle, draw a 24" square on a large piece of paper. (To adjust the finished length, begin with a larger or smaller square). Divide the square in half diagonally. Cut on all drawn lines. Each square will yield two triangles (Fig. 2). Cut as many triangles as you think you need, including the accent triangles.

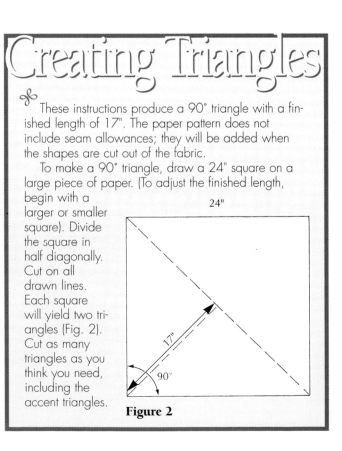

Figure 2

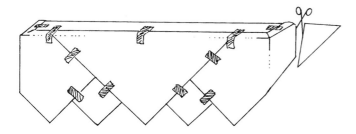

Figure 3

allowance around entire perimeter of triangle when cutting fabric! Cut lining triangles on opposite grain (Fig. 4b).

Figure 4

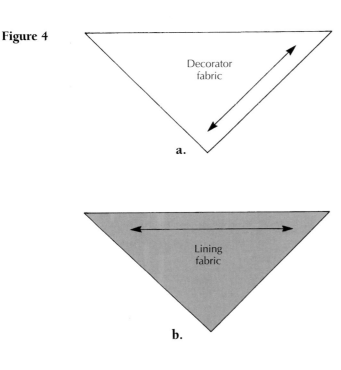

Decorator fabric

a.

Lining fabric

b.

2. Place decorator and lining fabrics right sides together. Stitch both diagonal sides. Trim the seam allowances to 1/4" to eliminate bulk. Clip the fabric diagonally at each point.

3. Turn the triangles right side out. Use a point turner to gently push fabric out from inside, and make sharp points. Press smooth.

4. On large work surface, arrange triangles right side up in planned configuration. Pin together. Stitch layers across top edge to secure.

5. Clean finish the top edge of valance by either serging, overcast stitching, or enclosing the raw edges in bias binding.

Installing the Valance

1. Remove mounting board from wall. Place valance on board; the upper edges of each triangle should overlap the board by 1/2". Use push pins to hold valance in place.

2. Staple valance to board; start in center and work toward each side. Miter the corners neatly to form the return (Fig. 5).

3. Place mounting board with attached triangles over angle brackets and screw brackets to board.

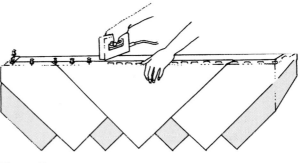

Figure 5

Alternative Design

Add tabs or a rod pocket and hang the valance on a decorative rod. This valance also looks super over the panel curtains on page 25.

Triangle Swag and Jabot

The swag-and-jabot window covering is a timeless treatment. Variations abound on this theme, but none are as easy to construct as this "triangle swag" and jabot. This treatment is adaptable to many sizes of windows— just add more triangle swags.

The swag (the triangle portion of the treatment) and the jabots (the pieces that cascade down the sides in delicate folds) are created separately and then stapled to a mounting board. The jabot is self-lined, while the swag is lined with lining fabric. The under treatment shown is an easy rod pocket panel curtain (see p. 25).

Techniques to Know Before You Begin

Materials Needed

From the Fabric Store
- Decorator fabric for swag, jabots, and panel curtains (Select medium-weight 54"- wide decorator fabrics, such as broadcloth, chintz, damask, linen, or sateen.)
- Lining fabric, 54" wide
- Thread to match decorator fabrics
- Dressmaker scissors
- Large pieces of paper for drafting pattern
- 1 1/8 yards of grosgrain ribbon, 1 1/8" wide

- Fabric marking pen or pencil
- Point turner
- Standard flat curtain rod (if using panel curtain)
- *Optional:* double-fold bias tape

From the Hardware Store
- 1 × 4" mounting board
- Angle brackets (at least 2, then one for every 36")
- Screws, 2" long (2–4 for each angle bracket)
- Heavy-duty staple gun with 1/2" staples
- Carpenter's square

Planning Your Valance

1. Determine the length of the mounting board. If window has a frame, measure the width of the window from outside frame edge to outside frame edge. Add 1" if not using side curtain panels; 2" if using side curtain panels. If the window does not have a frame, measure the opening and add 2" if not using side curtain panels; 3" if using side curtain panels.

2. Prepare mounting board either by painting it to match the wall color or by covering the board with decorator fabric.

3. Install mounting board 2 to 4" above the window like a shelf; use angle brackets to secure board to wall (Fig. 1). Note: Do not yet permanently attach the board to the brackets.

4. If you will use panel curtains with this valance, you need to plan for that

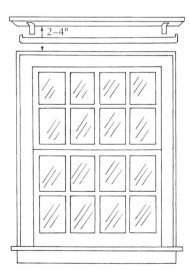

Figure 1

Possible Swag Measurements

Size of Square	Length of Diagonal	Drop Length of Swag
24"	34"	17"
25 1/2"	36"	18"
27"	38"	19"

rod placement at this time. Use a standard flat curtain rod, and mount it slightly below and just outside the angle brackets for the mounting board, as shown. When the valance and the curtains are installed, the sides and top of the panel curtains should be obscured by the valance.

5. Decide the number of triangle swags you would like on your valance. Keep in mind that an odd number of swags is usually more visually appealing than an even number. If more than one swag is used, you will need to overlap swags to fit the mounting board.

6. Determine the finished length of the triangle swags. Measure from the top edge of the mounting board to the point where you would like the swag to end. A good finished length is 17 to 19", but it can be any length that looks good on the window.

7. Make full-size paper patterns to determine the number of swags and the arrangement of the shapes, and to make adjustments to the suggested pattern dimensions. To do this, draw a square on the paper, at least 24". Divide the square in half diagonally to create a triangle shape (Fig. 2). Refer to "Possible Swag Measurements" to determine cutting dimensions. The pattern does not include the seam allowance—it will be added when the swag is cut out.

8. Simulate the jabots with paper patterns (use this pattern for visualization only—do not use the pattern to cut the fabric). Before cutting jabot shape, determine the long and short points of the jabot. A good short point is 14" and a good long point is 24", but they can be any lengths that look best on your window.

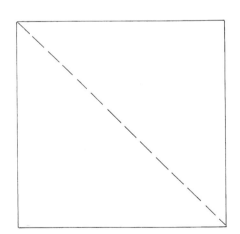

Figure 2

9. Hang the paper treatment to visualize the finished project. Remove the mounting board, use push pins to attach the paper swag and jabots to the board, and place the board back at window (Fig. 3). Stand back to see if you like the proportion to the window.

10. When you have determined the arrangement, make any notes that will help you during final installation. Remove the patterns and take them to the fabric store to determine the yardage needed. Match plaids,

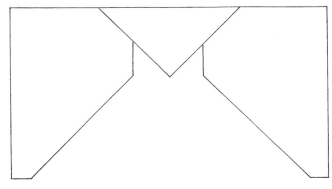

Figure 3

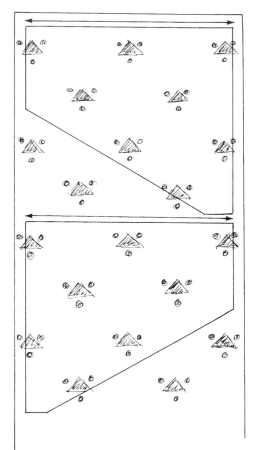

Figure 5

stripes, and motifs if necessary when planning fabric yardage.

11. Purchase fabric for jabots. Each jabot is self-lined. Therefore, you need 1½ yards (minimum) for each jabot. If the finished length of your jabots is greater than 24", you will need more fabric. Remember to include yardage to match repeats.

12. Purchase fabric for swags and the same amount of lining fabric for them.

Cutting Instructions

1. Using the swag paper pattern, cut shape(s) from the decorator and lining fabrics (Fig. 4). *Important:* Add ½" seam allowance around entire perimeter when cutting fabric!

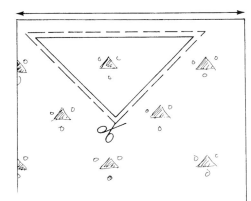

Figure 4
Before finalizing swag shape, consider the alternatives in Figures 12 and 13.

2. Use the full width of fabric, minus the selvages, for each jabot. Along one side edge, measure down the short point measurement plus 1". Mark. Along opposite edge, measure down the long point measurement plus 1". Mark. From this point, measure in from the edge 4" for the return. Mark. Connect all marks. Cut along all lines.

3. Cut out second jabot using the same measurements; make sure the right sides of the short points of the jabots are facing each

other (Fig. 5). (Avoid making two "left" or two "right" jabots.)

4. Cut the lining layers the same size and shape as the decorator fabrics.

Construction

Note: All seam allowances are ½" unless otherwise noted.

TRIANGLE SWAGS

1. Place decorator and lining fabrics right sides together. Stitch both diagonal sides. Trim the seam allowances to ¼" to eliminate bulk. Clip the fabric diagonally at each point (Fig. 6).

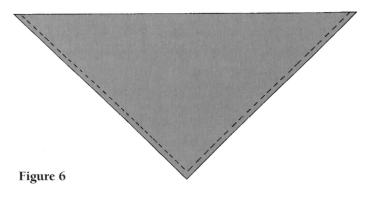

Figure 6

Shading Legend

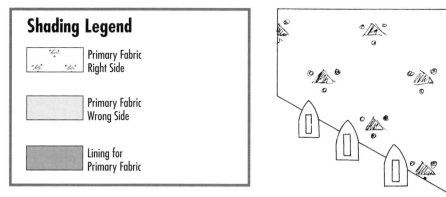

Primary Fabric
Right Side

Primary Fabric
Wrong Side

Lining for
Primary Fabric

2. Turn the triangles right side out. Use a point turner to gently push fabric out from inside, and make sharp points. Press smooth.

3. Clean finish top edge by either overcast stitching or enclosing the seam in bias tape.

JABOTS

1. Place decorator fabric and lining fabric right sides together. Stitch around three sides; leave top open for turning (Fig. 7). Trim the seam allowances to ¼" to eliminate bulk. Clip the fabric diagonally at each point.

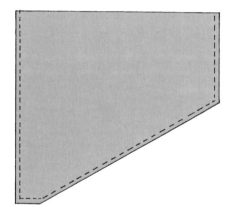

Figure 7

2. Turn the jabots right side out. Use a point turner to gently push fabric out from inside, and make sharp points. Press smooth.

TIP: When pressing the bias edges, avoid stretching the bias seams: First, position iron so that it is perpendicular to the crosswise grains of the fabric. Second, do not sweep the iron back and forth; instead, press by lifting your iron up and down (Fig. 8).

3. Gather the top edge of the jabot until the finished width is 24 to 36" (depending on the size of your window).

TIP: An easy way to gather fabric is to place unwaxed dental floss or strong cording ³⁄₈" from raw edges. Set machine to wide zigzag stitch.

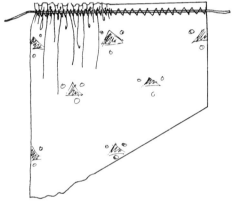

Figure 8

Stitch over cording; make sure cording is not caught in stitching. Gently pull floss or cording until gathers are evenly distributed (Fig. 9).

Figure 9

4. Use grosgrain ribbon to clean finish the top edge of the jabot. Pin ribbon to top edge of the decorator side of the jabots; stitch (Fig. 10). Clean finish the side edges of the ribbon by pressing cut edges under.

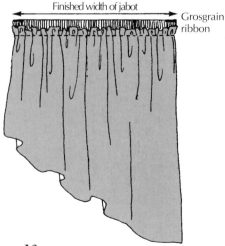
Finished width of jabot
Grosgrain ribbon

Figure 10

Installing the Valance

1. Arrange jabots at each end and around the return of the mounting board. Ribbon should overlap the top of the board by ¹/₂". Hold jabots temporarily in place with push pins until the you are pleased with the final arrangement (Fig. 11).

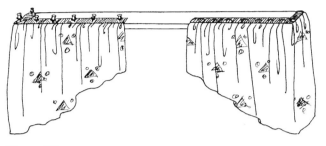

Figure 11

2. Arrange swag(s) as planned. The upper edges of each swag should overlap the board by ¹/₂". Hold the swags in place with push pins.

3. Staple units to board; start in center and work toward each side. Miter the corners neatly for the return.

4. Place mounting board over angle brackets and screw angle bracket to board.

Alternative Design

For two completely different looks, mount the jabots over the swag or change the shape of the swag from a point to a gently curving edge.

Alternative Swag Shape

For another type of jabot, cut shapes without a vertical short point. Construct swag as described.

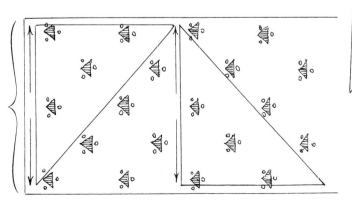

Figure 12

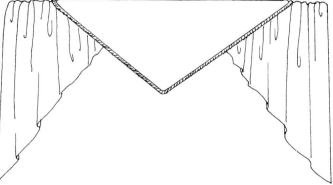

Figure 13

Chapter 5

GENERAL INSTRUCTIONS

General Instructions

Using this Chapter

Here's a table of contents showing what's included in this chapter. Reading the entire chapter is like taking a class in making window treatments. If you merely want to brush up on certain aspects of window treatments, choose from the subjects listed in the following box.

Some Terms to Know

Be sure you're familiar with these terms before beginning your project.

Apron—The bottom portion of the window frame that is flush against the wall.

Bias—Diagonal direction between the lengthwise and crosswise threads.

Cord cleat—A device on which the cord used to control adjustable window treatments (Roman or balloon shades, for example) is wrapped.

Crosswise grain—Threads that run perpendicular to the lengthwise grain and the selvage edge.

Cut length—The measurement of the fabric that equals the vertical length of the curtain or valance plus allowances for seams, take-up, headers, and hems.

Cut width—This is what the fabric should measure from side edge to side edge after fabric widths are sewn together and before any additional construction begins (such as side hems).

Decorator fabric—The main fabric in a window treatment. Also known as "face fabric" in the professional window covering industry.

Fabric panel—Term used to describe window treatment during construction process, after all widths are sewn together.

Finished length—The measurement equal to the vertical length of the treatment after all hems and pockets are sewn.

Finished width—The measurement of the fabric that equals the sum of the following: the horizontal length of the rod between brackets, plus the returns if any, plus yardage for the desired fullness needed to create the window treatment. It is the width of the fabric after all seams and side hems are sewn.

Fullness—The amount of fabric shirred, gathered, or pleated onto the rod to create the window treatment. Measure fullness by multiplying the length of the rod (sometimes plus the returns) by a number. The number depends on the style of window treatment.

Grain—See *Lengthwise grain* and *Crosswise grain*.

Header—The area of the window treatment above the rod pocket.

Heading—The area of the window treatment that includes the rod pocket and ruffle or fabric above the pocket.

Interlining—A third layer of fabric sandwiched between the decorator fabric and the lining that helps to deter light penetration and adds a layer of insulation for extreme temperature changes.

Length—Length can mean either the vertical measurement of a window treatment or the horizontal measurement of the drapery rod.

See also *Cut length* and *Finished length*.

Lengthwise grain—Fabric threads that are parallel to the selvage edge.

Level—A device used to determine if something is on the horizontal plane; if it is straight horizontally or vertically.

Mounting board—A 1-by-4", 1-by-6" or 1-by-8" piece of wood to which a valance is attached. It is mounted to the wall with angle brackets. Deeper boards are often used to mount valances over rod treatments.

Repeat—The distance from an element on one motif to the same element on the next along the selvage.

Return—The length of the end projection of the rod that extends out from the wall or the distance the bracket extends from the wall.

Self-lined—Using the same fabric to line a treatment as you use to make a treatment.

Selvages—The tightly woven finished lengthwise edges of the fabric.

Take-up—A situation that happens with a rod pocket curtain when the roundness of the rod forces the fabric to conform to the shape and the curtain is suddenly shorter. Think of when your blue jeans fit last year and after gaining a few pounds the jeans are shorter. Your leg is "taking up" the length.

Toggle bolt—A wall anchor that forms a brace inside the walls. It is generally used on hollow walls.

Width—See *Cut width* and *Finished width*.

Hints and Tips
WORKING EFFICIENTLY

• Set up a permanent work area for the duration of your project. Time and momentum are lost when you have to break down your work area after you finish each day.

• Work on as large a surface as possible. If using a dining room table, extend the table to its maximum size. If all else fails, move all the furniture and use the floor!

• Make sure you have a good light source in your work area.

• Keep all of your tools orderly and within reach.

• When sewing large volumes of fabric, keep the weight of the fabric from pulling on the needle by positioning a chair behind the sewing machine to "catch" the fabric as you sew.

• Wind three bobbins before you start a project; you will always have a spare at your fingertips.

• Start each project with a new needle; needles become dull through use. Select a needle that is compatible with the weight of your fabric (the needle package will provide you with this information). Needles break so always have extras on hand.

• Avoid eating and drinking in your work area. Spills and stains can be the downfall of any sewing project.

• Tidy up at the end of each work day; it's easier to get going when everything is in its place.

PLANNING YOUR WINDOW TREATMENT

• Some fabric stores have a policy that allows you to "check out" an entire bolt of fabric to see how it works in your home. If yours does, hang the fabric at the window and live with your choice for 24 hours. Look at the fabric in the morning, afternoon, and evening. Decide if you like it with the different sun exposure and with your furniture and other decor. If this isn't possible, purchase at least 1 yard. This small investment may save you money; you *may* change your mind about the fabric once you get it home. Also, by buying a small amount of fabric, you can do a "test-run" to see how the fabric sews, presses, and drapes.

• The construction area of headings and hems and all heading tapes should not be visible from outside the window. When deciding on hardware placement, make sure the rod is enough above the window opening to hide these details.

• To help you determine the perfect finished length of a valance, make a paper pattern and tape it to the window. Stand back and examine style, proportion, and length.

• Don't skimp on fullness. An expensive fabric will lose its impact if the treatment is not full enough. On the other hand, an inexpensive fabric will look rich if the fullness is abundant and if the window treatment is lined.

MEASURING

• Always mount the hardware before taking any measurements.

• Whenever possible, have all treatments in the same room hang from the same height. If window heights vary a few inches, use the highest window as the standard measurement. Raise the placement of the rods on the lower windows so that the window treatments are uniform.

• Windows in the same room may all *look* the same size; often, they are not. Measure each one and record its location in your notes.

• Floors can be uneven and windows out of plumb, so measure for the finished length in several places across the width of the window. Use the shortest measurement as the finished length, so the curtain doesn't buckle on the bottom edge. If the floor is carpeted, lay a

piece of cardboard over the carpet to get a more accurate measurement.

• If the distance between side-by-side windows is 12" or less, treat the area as one large window.

• For accurate measurements, be sure to use a stepladder to reach the top of the window. Use a retractable metal tape measure, not a cloth or plastic one; they stretch. Have someone else hold one end of the tape measure in position when taking measurements.

• Write down all measurements as you determine them. Create a grid like the "Measurement Log" so these figures are always close at hand.

• Check every measurement twice before cutting into the fabric!

FABRIC

• Consider the window treatment as a transition between indoors and outdoors. The fabric you select should harmonize not only with the room you are decorating, but also with the view from the window.

• Select the best quality fabric you can afford; the finished project will last longer and look better. To stretch your budget, consider using "seconds," a term that implies "second quality." Sometimes, however, fabric is classified a second simply because the color is slightly different from the company's standard. A knowledgeable salesperson can tell you why a second is classified as such.

• Before cutting into the fabric, check the entire yardage for flaws. If you find a simple thread flaw, and you can't cut around it, try to incorporate it into the headings or hems.

• Buy all the fabric you need for your project at the same time. Fabric is dyed in lots, and "dye lots" can vary significantly. If you run short of fabric, you may be able to find more, but not necessarily of the same dye lot.

• Generally, use fabrics that are manufactured for home-decorating projects. They have special finishes that prevent wrinkles and mildew and discourage insects; these finishes are what make these fabrics more expensive. Dress good fabrics do not have these finishes.

• If you know the window treatment will get unusually dirty, as in a kitchen or in a room with a wood stove, select a fabric that's intended to be washed.

• If necessary, preshrink before beginning your project. To preshrink your fabric, use the same method you will use to clean your project when it is finished. If you plan to launder the curtains, then launder the fabric. If you plan to dry clean your curtains, then have the dry cleaner preshrink the fabric. If you preshrink your fabric then preshrink all the components of the window treatment—

Measurement Log

	Top Layer	Top Layer Lining	Bottom Layer	Bottom Layer Lining
Cut Width				
Cut Length				
Finished Width				
Finished Length				
Number of Panels				
Yardage				
Also note your trim yardage				

trim, lining, drapery tapes, etc. (See Care and Cleaning, p. 94, before you decide.)

• Choose a thread color that is slightly darker than the predominant color in the fabric. Remember, you may need more than a single spool of thread for a large project.

STITCHING

• For all of the projects in this book, use a ½" seam allowance unless otherwise noted.

• To help sew a straight line, measure the appropriate distance from the needle and place a piece of masking tape on the machine bed. Use this as your seam guide.

• Stitch a few test seams to determine the correct stitch length for your fabric. If the seam puckers, try shortening the stitch length. A seam that puckers even slightly will prevent the drapery from hanging straight.

• Always place pins perpendicular to the edge of the fabric. Do not sew over the pins.

• Try not to lose pins inside the curtain—use glass-headed pins so they are easy to see.

• Backstitch at the beginning and end of each seam to secure the stitches in place. To backstitch, take a few stitches in reverse, then continue forward for the remainder of the seam.

• Do not overcast seam allowances unless it is specifically called for in the directions or unless it is absolutely necessary because of the type of fabric used. Each stitching line causes the fabric to draw up somewhat. Puckered seam allowances can result if the curtain is stitched too much. Also, overcasting can produce a ridge that may show through to the front after pressing.

• Always stitch from the bottom to the top.

This way if the fabric shifts and loses its match, the mismatched area will fall into the heading area where it won't be as noticeable.

PRESSING

When making professional-looking window treatments, the correct pressing technique is just as important as taking accurate measurements.

• Give your iron a thorough cleaning before starting your project.

• Use a press cloth to prevent scorch and iron shine.

• Use a scrap piece of fabric to test your fabric for the perfect temperature. Check to see if there are press marks, if the finish is damaged, or if water spots are visible. Determine if you get better results with a dry iron and a moist press cloth or a steam iron and a dry press cloth. If using a steam iron, do not overfill—unwanted splashes on fabric can be disastrous.

• The amount of fabric required to make some window treatments can be cumbersome. A traditional ironing board is too small to accommodate this amount of fabric. The solution? Create your own surface. Rest a door or a sheet of plywood on two sawhorses. Cut a piece of muslin that's a foot or so larger on all sides than the surface. Place several wool or cotton blankets (no polyester) on the surface and cover with the muslin. Pull the muslin taut, and secure the edges of it to the underside of the door or plywood. Voila!

• To achieve crisp edges when pressing a lined curtain, first press the seam open.

Then, arrange the panel so that the lining and decorator fabrics are equally divided and neither show on the opposite side. Press again if necessary.
• Press by lifting the iron up and down. "Sweeping" the iron back and forth stretches the bias edges and the seams.
• Press on the wrong side of the fabric when possible. If you must press on the right side of the fabric, always use a press cloth.
• To prevent seam lines from appearing on the surface, place a strip of brown craft paper between the seam allowance and the fabric. Remove the paper after the seams are pressed.

CARE AND CLEANING
• Always work with clean hands during the construction process.
• Regular vacuuming will remove dust and pollen. Pay particular attention to pleats and gathers, where dust collects.
• Hang your window treatments outside on a dry breezy day to help keep the fabrics clean and fresh. Alternatively, place a curtain panel and a damp—not wet—cloth into the dryer. Turn the dryer on "air fluff" and tumble for about 15 minutes. The tumbling action shakes the dirt and dust free, and the cloth absorbs these impurities.
• As a last resort, take your curtains to the dry cleaner. Be aware that some of the protective fabric finishes may be removed during the cleaning process. This may result in the fabrics being less crisp and without some of the protection against stains or sun. Check with friends or a local decorator for their recommendations for dry cleaners. Keep a record of the finished size, fabric finishes, fiber content, and manufacturer's care instructions, and provide your dry cleaner with this information.
• If the window treatments are the same size in the same room, rotate them periodically from window to window. Because different windows get different sun exposure, this prevents one treatment from wearing out or fading before another.

HARDWARE
• Buy good-quality hardware from a reputable manufacturer. Don't try to save money by buying bargain brands; they usually aren't sturdy enough.
• Ideally, mount hardware at each window before beginning your window treatment; hardware dimensions may affect your yardage calculations (especially with rod-pocket treatments).
• Enlist a partner to help you install drapery hardware. Two sets of eyes are better than one

when deciding on placement, and two sets of hands make the installation easier.
• If placing hardware over an existing treatment that will remain in place, allow for necessary clearance between the layers. This same guideline applies when installing a soft treatment over existing vertical or horizontal blinds. Remember to allow room to manipulate the blinds.
• The curtain rod must be level for the window treatment to hang straight. The only way to determine if the rod is truly straight is to use a carpenter's level.
• The most secure place to mount your hardware is into a stud. The structure of a house usually dictates that wooden 2-by-4s surround each window opening. The easiest way to find these studs is to knock firmly on the wall with the heel of your clenched fist. A solid sound means you have located a stud; a hollow sound tells you to keep knocking. Once you've found the studs, mark them at the level you plan to hang the brackets.

Before You Begin
Here is a review of some of the techniques used in this book. These how-to's will help you create beautiful window treatments that will dazzle your friends and family, and make your home look sensational!

YARDAGE CALCULATIONS
Careful calculation of yardage is essential when making window treatments. The yardage formulas in this book were developed specifically for each window treatment. I suggest recording your calculations as you determine them.
Here's an example of a yardage calculation to show you the complete process—this one's for the Cuffed Curtain.
Let's say the distance between the two brackets is 42", the distance from the bottom of the rings to the floor is 85", and the fabrics used are 54" wide with a 27" repeat. The cut length of the contrasting cuff is 13", and also has a 27" repeat.
1. Install the rod according to manufacturer's instructions.
2. To determine the finished width, measure the rod from bracket to bracket—42". Multiply this number by 2½ for adequate fullness—42" × 2½ = 105".
3. To determine the cut width of the fabric, add 4" to above measurement for side hems—105 + 4" = 109".
4. To determine the number widths you need to construct the curtain, divide the cut width by the width of fabric you are using—109" ÷ 54" = 2.01, rounded to 2.

5. To determine the cut length of the fabric widths, place several rings onto the rod. Measure from the bottom edge of the ring to the floor. If the floor is carpet-covered, lay a piece of cardboard over the carpet to get an accurate measurement. Add 8½" for the hem and seam allowance. Design option: If you want to "puddle" the curtain on the floor as I did, add an additional 12 to 15". This is the cut length of the fabric panels—85" + 8½ + 15 = 108½".

6. To determine the yardage, multiply the cut length by the number of widths needed from Step 4—108½" × 2 = 217". If the fabric has a repeat, multiply the repeat distance by number of widths and add this figure to the total. The extra fabric added to each width will allow you to match the designs—27" × 2 = 54" + 217" = 271". Divide this number by 36—271" ÷ 36 = 7.52 yards. Add additional fabric for facing. You need one facing strip for every width of fabric needed to construct the curtain. Facing is cut 5" by number of widths of fabric—5" × 2 = 10", or .27 yard. Add yardage for panels and yardage for facing—7.52 yards + .27 = 7.79 yards. For total yardage, round total up to the next ¼ yard—8 yards.

7. Calculate again for lining; do not include fabric needed for repeat or for facing—217" ÷ 36 = 6.02, round up to next ¼ yard—6¼ yards.

8. Here's how to determine the total yardage for the contrasting cuff. You need the same number of widths for the cuff as you do for the curtain—2. Multiply the cut length by the number of widths needed—13" × 2 = 26". If the fabric has a repeat, add the repeat distance to the total. The extra fabric added will allow you to match the designs—27" + 26 = 53". Divide this number by 36 and round up to next ¼ yard—53" ÷ 36 = 1.47 yards rounded to 1½ yards.

9. Calculate again for lining of the cuff; do not include yardage for the repeat—13" × 2 = 26" ÷ 36 = .72 yard rounded up to .75, or ³/₄ yard.

Straightening Fabric

In theory, fabric needs to be perfectly "on grain", or straight, for the project to be perfect. The grain of fabric refers to the direction of the threads. Being on grain means that the crosswise threads are perpendicular to the lengthwise threads, and that the fabric is straight. This is particularly important for patterned fabrics. If the pattern is noticeably off-grain, your treatment will appear askew.

Few fabrics are printed precisely on grain. To ensure that the fabric was straight, sewers traditionally pulled a crosswise

thread the entire width of the fabric, and then cut on this newly defined line. Today however, many decorator fabrics have finishes applied to the surface. Consequently, the threads are locked in place and can not be manipulated. So follow these instructions to straighten your fabric.

1. Work on a large, flat surface.

2. Unroll several yards of fabric, right side up. Bring the selvages together, and fold the fabric so that it lies flat. For patterned fabric, make sure the motifs match. Make a small snip with scissors in the selvage area through both layers, close to the unfinished edge.

3. Open the fabric to a single thickness, right side up. At the snip, align the short blade of the carpenter's square with one selvage of the fabric (Fig. 1). Using the other blade as a straightedge, draw a line across the fabric beginning at the snip. Continue this line across the width of the fabric. Move the carpenter's square in 12" increments (the line will be straight if the carpenter's square is extended no more than 12" at a time).

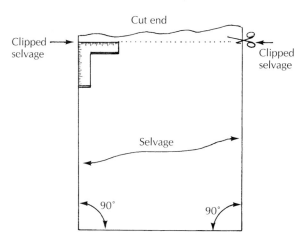

Figure 1

4. Ideally, the line will be at a perfect right angle to the selvage, and the line will meet the snip at the opposite selvage edge. If it is just slightly off-grain—if where the line meets the selvage is ¾" or less from the snip—and the fabric is tightly woven, it is more important to follow the pattern and not the grain. However, if the difference is more than ¾", consider using another fabric. (It's best to treat an all-over, non-obvious print as a solid.)

5. Cut along the drawn line.

Note: Stripes, plaids and solids are most obvious if printed off grain. To avoid this problem, choose a fabric that is woven, not printed. A woven fabric looks the same on both sides whereas a printed fabric has an obvious right and wrong side.

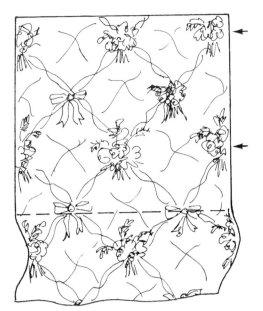

Figure 3

CUTTING FABRIC LENGTHS

Note: Before cutting into your fabric, determine its direction or top edge by studying the design. The direction of a design with flowers, stems, and leaves is easy to discern but other fabric designs may not be so obvious. However, many fabrics have a directional arrow printed on the selvage to help you determine the direction of the print.

1. From the straightened end, measure the cut length along the selvage, and mark the cut length.

2. Using a straightedge, draw a line across the width of the fabric. With a carpenter's square, check to see if the line is straight. Cut along the drawn line. This is the first squared-off length.

3. To cut additional lengths, use the first length as a guide and place it directly on top of remaining fabric; match motifs.

4. Use a straight edge to mark the cutting line (Fig. 2).

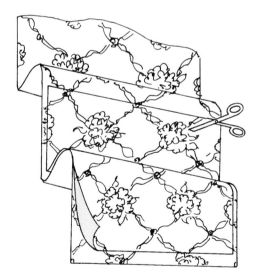

Figure 2

5. After each panel is cut, snip a small corner off the top of each panel, so you can quickly distinguish between the top and the bottom of the panels.

WHAT IS A REPEAT?

Patterned fabrics have motifs or designs that repeat uniformly. A "repeat" is the length of one full motif; it is the distance from an element on the motif to the same element on the next motif. When looking for the repeat, examine the selvage. Find a distinguishing feature of the printed motif and scan the fabric downward for the next, same feature (Fig. 3). The distance can vary from 1 to 36".

If your fabric has a prominent repeat design, you must determine where the design falls on the finished panel. Regardless of how many window treatments are in the same room, they must be cut so the horizontal repeat is in the same position. Use these rules to determine where the motif should fall.

• For floor-length panels, place one full repeat just below the heading; it's where the eye travels first.

• For sill-length panels, the repeat placement is just the reverse—one full repeat ends at the hem.

• If you have floor- and sill-length window treatments in the same room, follow the floor-length guideline.

MATCHING REPEATS

On professional window treatments, the repeats match at all seams. Extra fabric is needed to accomplish this. Each set of instructions in this book includes how to calculate the extra yardage, but the rule is allow one repeat for each cut length of fabric.

If you are having trouble matching the motifs in your fabric don't despair. The easy solution is to "fuse-baste" the seams by using a paper-backed fusible tape. It's essential to use a tape that can be stitched through; other types of tape can damage your sewing machine.

1. Lay full width of fabric on large work surface, wrong side down.

2. Lay the additional panel along the appropriate side of the first width, also wrong side down; align motifs. Press under the inside edge of the joining panel toward wrong side—about ⅝" (Fig. 4a).

3. Place a strip of paper-backed fusible tape,

adhesive side down, close to pressed under edge of the joining panel, as shown in Fig. 4b. Set iron in the maximum steam range suitable for fabric. Place iron on the paper side; allow to cool, then remove paper.

4. Lap pressed seam allowance over the unpressed one; match motifs exactly. Pin in place. Fuse the two layers together.

5. Arrange the panels right sides together. Stitch directly in creased line. The motif will be perfectly matched!

6. Trim seam allowance to ½".

STITCHING FABRIC WIDTHS TOGETHER

The cut width measurement is sometimes wider than the fabric you have chosen. It is then necessary to sew widths of fabric together to achieve the cut width measurement. If you were to simply sew two widths together, you would create a center seam—a telltale sign that your treatment is "homemade". Here are tips to avoid a center seam.

• If you need 1½ widths, cut one panel in half lengthwise and stitch one half width to one outside edge of the full width (Fig. 5).

• If you need two widths of fabric, cut one width in half lengthwise and stitch one half width to each side of the full width (Fig. 6).

• If you need three full widths of fabric, stitch the widths together side by side (Fig. 7). This arrangement does not result in a center seam.

ADVANTAGES OF LINING WINDOW TREATMENTS

There are many advantages of lining window treatments. While you'll incur some additional cost and invest a little more time, lining extends the life of the window treatment, enhances its appearance, increases insulation and makes light to medium-weight fabrics hang better. Lining provides a little more privacy and cuts down on the amount of light, noise, and dust that filter through a window. Also, lining hides construction details and, if it is all the same color, gives windows a unified appearance on the outside.

Select fabrics designed specifically for lining. Lining fabrics are a durable fiber or a blend of fibers that is resistant to sunlight deterioration. Usually these fabrics are cotton or cotton/polyester blends and many have protective finishes that will contribute to the durability of the window treatment. White and off-white are the two most popular colors, but if the lining will show on the front and is part of the overall design, consider using a coordinating color. If you choose a fabric other than standard lining fabric, it

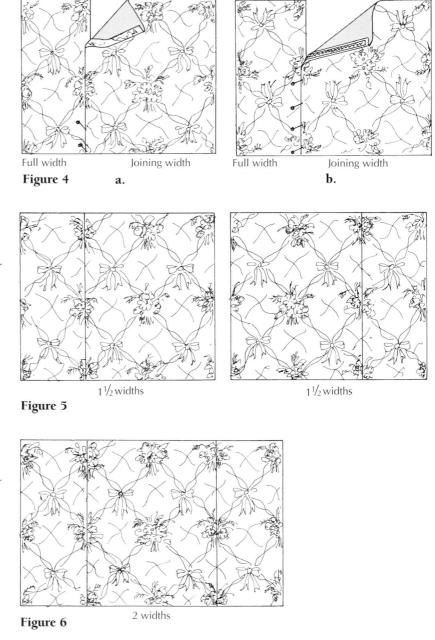

Full width   Joining width   Full width   Joining width

Figure 4   **a.**   **b.**

1½ widths   1½ widths

Figure 5

2 widths

Figure 6

3 widths

Figure 7

must be compatible with the decorator fabric. It must be the same width, the same or lighter weight, and have the same care requirements.

HEMS

Custom-made curtains, draperies, and valances have double hems at the bottom. Side hems are also double-hemmed (1 to 2") unless they are incorporated into a "pillow-cased" lining, as is done often in this book. Double hems are double the thickness of a single hem.

In this book the bottom hem for floor-length curtains is a double 4" hem. However, if your fabric is heavy, you may want to increase this to a double 5" or even 6" hem. The bottom hem of a valance can be a double 2 or 3" hem. When possible, hem the bottom first, and then the sides. This will assure a clean finish along the bottom side edge because the folds in the hem will not show. The lining hem is usually 1" narrower than the hem on the decorator fabric. For example, if bottom hem of a fabric panel is a double 4" hem, the lining is a double 3" hem. For bottom hems, always hem the lining and decorator fabric separately.

For example, to create a double 4" hem at the bottom of a decorator fabric panel, fold over and press 8" of fabric toward the wrong side. Next, tuck in the top of the hem 4" to meet the fold. Stitch or fuse hem (Fig. 8). To hem the lining fabric, create a double 3" hem. Fold over and press 6" of fabric toward the wrong side. Next, tuck in the top of the hem 3" to meet the fold. Stitch or fuse hem.

For a professional finish for formal window treatments, blind stitch the hems. If the blind stitch leaves a visible crease on the front of the window treatment, take smaller "bites" into the decorator fabric or loosen the top tension slightly. If the fabric shifts when stitching a blind hem, hand baste the hem in place first.

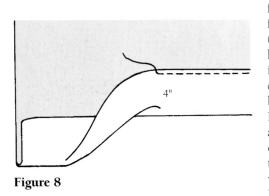

Figure 8

MAKING SMOOTH CURVES

Curved edges or shapes make window treatments interesting. When sewing a curved edge, use a short stitch length and stitch slowly and accurately; the seam allowance must be consistent in width. For curved edges to lie flat, the seam allowances must be graded and then clipped and/or notched.

Grading refers to a method of trimming seam allowances. To grade, trim each layer of the seam allowance to a different width. Grade seam allowances when they are turned in the same direction, as opposed to pressed open or flat. Generally, trim the seam allowance of the lining or contrasting fabric more than the seam allowance of the decorator fabric so that the seam allowance of the decorator fabric is wider than the seam allowance of the lining fabric (Fig. 9).

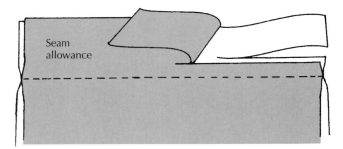

Seam allowance

Figure 9

After seams are graded, they are clipped and/or notched at regular intervals (Fig. 10). Clipping refers to making a snip into the seam allowance; notching means cutting small wedges from the seam allowance. On an outward curve, notch the seam allowance. On an inward curve, clip the seam allowance. Be careful to clip and notch to, but not through, the stitching line.

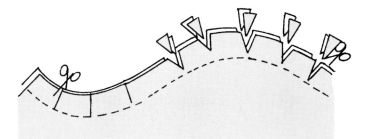

Figure 10

TURNING A CORNER

Turning a corner precisely creates a sharply defined point or edge.
1. When you come to a corner or point, leave the needle down in the fabric, raise the presser foot, rotate the fabric, lower the presser foot, and continue stitching (Fig. 11).
2. Due to the nature of some fabrics, corners and points may be distorted. This is often the case with loosely woven, stretchy, or very

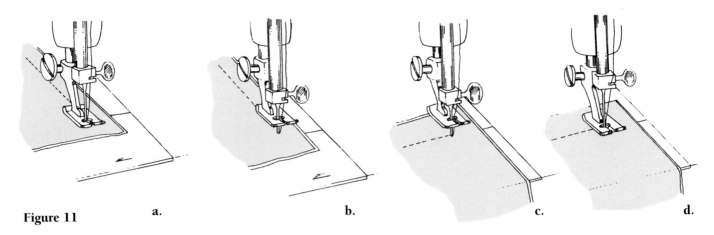

Figure 11   **a.**   **b.**   **c.**   **d.**

heavy fabrics. To keep the corners square, "blunt" the corners. For lightweight fabrics, take one stitch diagonally across the corner (Fig. 12a), two on medium-weight fabrics (Fig. 12b), and three on heavy fabrics (Fig. 13). For added reinforcement stitch again directly over first stitching line at each corner.

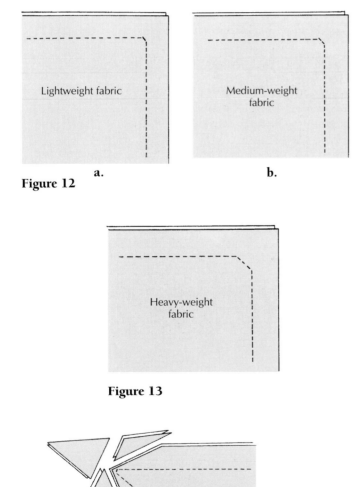

Figure 12   **a.**   **b.**

Figure 13

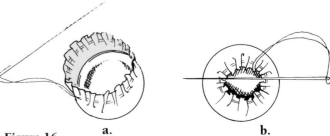

Figure 14

3. To eliminate bulk, clip corners diagonally (Fig. 14). Next, taper the seam allowances away from the corner; the sharper the point, the further the seam allowance must be trimmed.

4. Turn right sides out. Using a point turner, gently push the fabric out from the inside to create sharp points. Press the seam so neither the lining nor the decorator fabric shows on the opposite side.

COVERING BUTTONS

Covered buttons are a wonderful finishing touch for many of the window treatments in this book. Commercial kits are available that make this process easy. Still, you may find these steps helpful when covering your buttons.

1. Cut a circle of fabric using the pattern that is included with the button forms.

2. Hand sew a row of running stitches around the outside edge of the circle (Fig. 15). Leave the needle and thread attached to the fabric at the end of stitching.

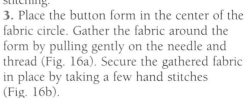

Figure 15

3. Place the button form in the center of the fabric circle. Gather the fabric around the form by pulling gently on the needle and thread (Fig. 16a). Secure the gathered fabric in place by taking a few hand stitches (Fig. 16b).

Figure 16   **a.**   **b.**

4. Place the button back over the button front; make sure all fabric edges are between button front and back and the fabric is smooth over the front and around the edges. **5.** Use the tool provided with the kit to snap the button into place.

MAKE YOUR OWN PIPING

Cording and piping are both types of trim. The terms are often used interchangeably, but there is a difference. The filler of piping is thin; the filler of cording is thick. You can purchase both styles, but the color range is limited. To ensure a perfect match, make your own; it's easier than you think! (There are two methods for covering cording or piping. After this general set of instructions, directions for both follow.)

Note: For ease of understanding, we'll use "cording" to refer to both cording and piping in the following directions.

1. Select the cord diameter from an assortment of sizes.
2. Bias strips of fabric are used to cover the cord. The cut width of the strip depends on the diameter of the cord and the weight of the fabric. The strip needs to be wide enough to wrap around the cord plus form a 1/2" seam allowance.
3. Make a template for the bias strip pieces. Fold a corner of fabric or tissue paper around the cord and encase the cord snugly. Pin to secure. Measure 1" out from the pin and cut (Fig. 17). Use this template to cut bias strips.

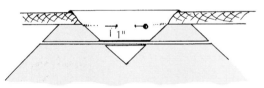

Figure 17

4. Select a method for cutting bias strips—either the continuous bias method or single strip method. Again, directions follow.
5. After bias strips are cut and pieced together, press the entire length of the strip. Stretch the fabric slightly as you press it to ensure the covering will be smooth.
6. Lay cord in the center of the wrong side of the fabric. Fold fabric around the cord with raw edges even.
7. Attach zipper foot or special piping foot to your sewing machine, following manufacturer's instructions. Stitch close to the cord (Fig. 18). The stitching line should not be extremely tight against the cord. Any extra space will be used when the piping is

Figure 18

sewn to the decorator fabric. Trim seam allowances to 1/2".

Directions for Continuous Bias Strips
Note: Continuous bias strips are best if you need large quantities of piping. Approximately 26 yards of 1³/4"-wide bias strips can be cut from one yard of 54"-wide fabric; 20 yards of 2¹/4"-wide strips.
1. Straighten one edge of fabric using a carpenter's square.
2. Next, take the cut edge to the selvage at a 45° angle (Fig. 19). Finger press at each corner of folded section to mark bias edge.

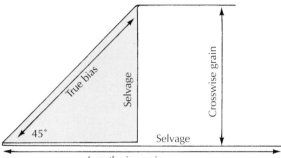

Figure 19

3. With a fabric pen or pencil and straightedge, draw a line that connects these two marks. Cut carefully along line (Fig. 20).
4. Move the fabric triangle you have cut to the other end of the fabric. Arrange fabric as shown in Fig. 21. Place right sides together and stitch the two pieces together; use 1/4" seam allowance. Press seam.

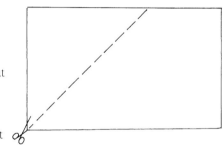

Figure 20

5. On wrong side of fabric, draw lines parallel to the bias edge the width you need for your project (Fig. 22); use the template from Step 3 in Make Your Own Piping.
6. Arrange fabric so right side bias edges meet; match drawn lines. Note: Offset the

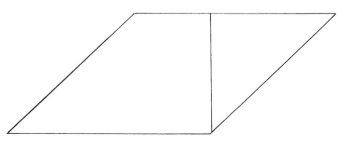

Figure 21

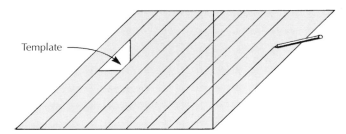

Figure 22

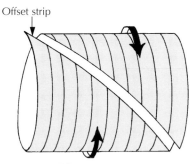

Offset strip

Figure 23

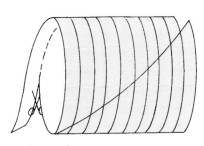

Figure 24

fabric so a strip extends to one side. If one strip is not offset (see Fig. 23), you will make bias circles instead of bias strips. Stitch bias edges together; use 1/4" seam allowance. Press seam allowances to one side.

7. Cut along drawn lines with scissors (Fig. 24) until entire tube is transformed into one long bias strip.

Directions for Single Cut Bias Strips

1. Straighten one edge of fabric using a carpenter's square.

2. Next, take the cut edge to the selvage at a 45° angle. Finger press at each corner of folded section to mark bias edge.

3. Use the template from Step 3 in Make Your Own Piping to draw parallel lines to the folded edge (Fig. 25). At each end, draw a line parallel to the selvage. Cut along all drawn lines.

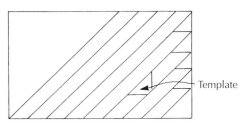

Template

Figure 25

4. Place strips right sides together at a right angle; offset tips slightly so cut edges match at the seam lines. Stitch strips together with a 1/4" seam allowance (Fig. 26). Continue sewing strips together in this way until you have one long strip. Press seam allowances to one side. Trim ends.

Figure 26

WORKING WITH PURCHASED TRIMS

Purchased trims can add an elegant touch to home-decorating projects, especially window treatments. The types of trim used in this book are brush fringe, cording, and piping. The brush fringe and piping adorn the bottom edge of the Flip-Over Valance. Tabs are made from cording in several window treatments.

Brush fringe is made of cut yarn that is fastened together along one edge. It is available in a variety of lengths and thicknesses. The fringe usually comes with a row of stitching along the fringe edge, to keep it neat. Leave the stitching in place until the project is complete, then pull the stitching away to free the fringe.

When incorporating fringe into seam allowances, place the fringe between two layers of fabric with the free ends away from the seam line. Be sure to incorporate the header of the trim—the area above the stitching that keeps the trim together— into the seam allowance. If the seam puckers, clip the header at regular intervals. Be careful to not clip through the stitching line.

Decorative cording will fray once it is cut. To prevent this, wrap transparent tape around the section to be cut, and then cut through the middle of the tape (Fig. 27). Leave the tape in place until you have used the cording in your project.

USING DRAPERY WEIGHTS

Specially designed drapery weights will ensure that your window treatments hang well. First, cover the weight with muslin to prevent the

Tape

Figure 27

Add drapery weight in
corner of hem

Figure 28

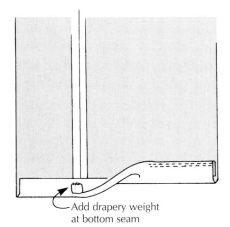

Add drapery weight
at bottom seam

Figure 29

weight from discoloring the decorator fabric. Then, insert the weight into the hem area at each corner (Fig. 28) and/or at each vertical seam (Fig. 29).

USING DRAPERY TAPES
Ring Tape

Using ring tape has several advantages when constructing a Roman shade: The tape strengthens the shade and will save you the aggravation of measuring exact intervals between rings. To eliminate the stitching lines on the outside of the Roman shade, use iron-on ring tape instead of the sew-in ring tape. If using iron-on ring tape, secure lining to decorator fabric with fusible tape. Place fusible tape directly on each planned ring tape line.

Pleater Tape

Traditionally, pinch pleats were painstakingly marked and hand stitched in place. However, today you can buy specially developed tapes that arrange the fabric into a series of regularly spaced pleats quickly and easily.

Multi-pleater tape is exactly as the name suggests. The tape is woven with pre-spaced

pockets into which you insert "fingers" of hooks. The multiple pockets can be spaced as desired and are used effectively to create cluster pleats.

The perfect pleater tape makes crisp pleats that are evenly spaced every time. Fold the section into pleats on the broken lines and insert the special clamp that holds the pleat in place.

INSTALLING A MOUNTING BOARD

1. Prepare the board either by painting it to match the wall color or by covering the board with decorator fabric. If you choose to cover it, wrap the board as if you are wrapping a package, and staple the fabric to the underside of the board to hold it in place.
2. Mark screw placement for angle brackets on the bottom of board. Drill screw holes into board; the size of the hole is determined by the size of screw you are using. Screw brackets to board. To prevent the threads of the fabric from twisting around the screw on a fabric-covered mounting board, make a pilot hole through the fabric and into the board with an awl.

3. The most secure place to mount your hardware is into a stud. Usually, wooden 2-by-4s surround a window opening. The easiest way to find a stud is to knock firmly on the wall with the heel of your fist. A solid sound means you have located a stud. Once you've found the studs, mark the wall where you intend to place the brackets.

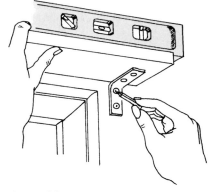

Figure 30

4. Position the board and make sure the board is level. Mark the exact position of screw holes on the wall (Fig. 30).
5. Remove the angle brackets from the board and secure the brackets to the wall (Fig. 31).

If you are going directly into a stud, the recommended screws to use are drywall screws. If you cannot secure the screws into studs, choose either spreading anchors or toggle bolts.

A spreading anchor consists of a bolt and

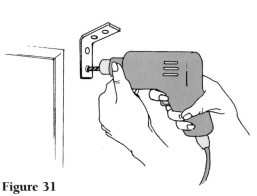

Figure 31

metal sleeve. The anchor is tapped into a predrilled hole. Tighten the bolt and the sleeve expands against the backside of the wall. Next, remove the bolt, slip it through the hole in the bracket and retighten the bolt in the sleeve.

Toggle bolts have spring-loaded, winglike toggles that expand after they have been pushed through the wall. Drill a hole large enough for the compressed toggles. Pass the bolt through the hole in the bracket and screw it into the toggles. Slide the toggles through the hole. Tighten the bolt and the toggles will open and pull up against the back of the wall.

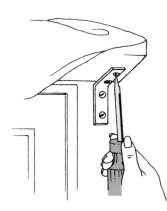

Figure 32

6. Place mounting board with attached window treatment over angle brackets and screw brackets to board. Hold board in place with clamps when screwing angle bracket to board (Fig. 32).

INSTALLING RODS AND BRACKETS

1. Hold the end brackets where desired on the window; mark the screw locations by poking a pencil through the screw holes in each bracket. Remember—the most secure place to mount your hardware is into a stud (see Hardware on p. 94).

2. Using the screw-hole marks as a guide, drill holes for the screws (for plaster or studs) or the wall anchors (which help anchor the screws in drywall) into wall. The size of the drill bit depends on the size of the screw or wall anchor used.

3. If using wall anchors, tap the anchor into the wall with a hammer. Then tighten the screw so the wall anchor expands.

4. Remove the screw from the wall anchor. Place the screw in the bracket screw hole. Align the screw with the wall anchor, and screw the bracket in place.

5. If installing an extra-long ride, or bracket, additional supports may need to be installed to help support the weight of the window treatment.

ENLARGING PATTERNS FROM GRIDDED DIAGRAMS

1. On a large piece of tracing paper (available in office supply stores), draw a grid of squares that are equal to the grid size indicat-

ed on the small diagrams (usually 1"). You can also buy 1" grid paper at art supply stores and some office supply stores.

2. Carefully copy the pattern, one square at a time, onto the large grid. The result should be a full-size paper pattern.

3. Follow the specific project instructions for adding seam allowances.

Checklist for Quality Window Treatments

❑ Plan window treatments with adequate fullness. This means a cut width up to $2\frac{1}{2}$ to 3 times the width of the window. Purchase ample fabric.

❑ Cut off all selvages to prevent puckering and see through the selvage markings.

❑ Match pattern repeats at all possible seams. When more than one patterned window treatment hangs in a room, the pattern repeat must be at the same place on all of them.

❑ Insert drapery weights in all corners and seams to ensure the window treatment hangs smoothly.

❑ Line all window treatments. Neutral, white, and off-white are the best colors for lining fabrics. Press carefully so the lining cannot be seen from the front.

❑ Make sure all stitching lines are as inconspicuous as possible, especially bottom and side hems.

❑ The bottom hems of floor-length curtains are at least a double 4" hem. Linings are 1" shorter than decorator panels. Hem decorator panels and lining panels separately at the bottom.

❑ All sides are double-hemmed 1 to 2".

❑ Blind stitch hems with a monofilament (clear) thread or a thread that matches the fabric.

❑ Miter the corners where the bottom and the side hems meet; hand sew them with small blind stitches.

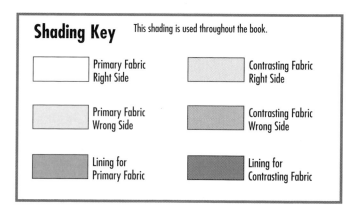

Shading Key   This shading is used throughout the book.

☐	Primary Fabric Right Side	☐	Contrasting Fabric Right Side
☐	Primary Fabric Wrong Side	☐	Contrasting Fabric Wrong Side
☐	Lining for Primary Fabric	☐	Lining for Contrasting Fabric

Index